ENGLISH EXAMINED

TO EXAMINE: To make enquiry into; to search into;
to scrutinise. 'When I began to examine the extent and
certainty of our knowledge, I found it had a near connexion with words' (Locke).

Dr Johnson's fifth definition

ENGLISH EXAMINED

Two centuries of comment on the mother-tongue

COMPILED AND INTRODUCED

BY

SUSIE I. TUCKER

ARCHON BOOKS
1974

Library of Congress Cataloging in Publication Data

Tucker, Susie I   comp.
  English examined; two centuries of comment on the mother-tongue.

  Reprint of the ed. published by the Cambridge University Press.
  Includes bibliographical references.
    1. English language—History—Addresses, essays, lectures.   2. English language — Grammar, Historical.   I. Title.
PE1072.T82   1974   420'.9   74-4193
ISBN 0-208-01427-6

© 1961 Cambridge University Press
First published 1961
Reprinted 1974 by permission of Cambridge
University Press in an unabridged and
unaltered edition as an Archon Book,
an imprint of The Shoe String Press, Inc.,
Hamden, Connecticut 06514

Printed in the United States of America

The chief End, proposed by the Author of this Treatise in making it public, has been to excite his Readers to curiosity and inquiry; not to teach them himself by prolix and formal lectures . . . but to induce them . . . to become Teachers to themselves, by an impartial use of their own understandings. He thinks nothing more absurd than the common notion of Instruction, as if Science were to be poured into the Mind, like water into a cistern, that passively waits to receive all that comes. The growth of Knowledge he rather thinks to resemble the growth of Fruit; however external causes may in some degree co-operate, 'tis the internal vigour, and virtue of the tree, that must ripen the juices to their just maturity.

From Harris's Preface to *Hermes*, 1751

CONTENTS

Contents

Contents

ix

Contents

Contents

Contents

Contents

Contents

Contents

Contents

PREFACE

This collection of comments on English from about 1600 to soon after 1800 is the outcome of some twenty-five years' experience of trying to make undergraduates aware that a study of their mother tongue is both relevant and interesting.

There are two main difficulties. One is to bring home to the students who are in no way philologists (and they are the majority) a sense of the inter-relations between both language and literature, and language and life; the other is to prevent their knowledge from being merely second-hand, drawn from books on the history of the language but not from their own first-hand investigation.

In view of the breadth and weight of honours courses in English, it would be over-optimistic to expect students to hunt out material in the stack-room of the library, or even in its locked cases, and this is a difficulty which I feel a collection of extracts in handy form may go a long way to meet.

The Critique of Pure English (Society of Pure English Tract No. LXV) is invaluable so far as it goes: but it is largely restricted to vocabulary; it represents the eighteenth century by two passages only: and it suffers from the insuperable defect of being out of print. It is of course available for reference in libraries, so I have tried to avoid overlapping with it.

To avoid quoting at length from easily accessible books, I have left out some of the most important names in English linguistic criticism, or represented them barely: but I have added in Appendix I lists of key passages to indicate the topics dealt with and the books where they may be most conveniently found. In Appendix II, I have sorted out passages of directly linguistic comment from Spingarn's *Critical Essays of the 17th Century*, and Durham's similar book for the eighteenth.[1]

I have tried to represent the views of speakers and writers of English during the seventeenth and eighteenth centuries and a few from the early nineteenth century on as many aspects of the language as possible —its historical relations, its development, its pronunciation, its vocabulary, its forms, its grammar, its standards and aberrations; that perpetual bone of contention, its spelling; its diffusion overseas: its past and its future. And I have called for comment from all sorts and conditions of

[1] *Critical Essays of the Eighteenth Century.*

men, in order to show that it is a matter of deep human interest. It would be ungrateful and absurd to fall in with Defoe's prejudices and exclude professional scholars: but the professional scholar and his scientific study of English can easily overwhelm the student, who is not likely to be enthusiastic about morphemes, phonemes and semantemes, and may all too easily conclude that these terms of art belong to a discipline which is not for him. So my authorities are people of varied interests. We have John Wallis, who wrote an English grammar but was a mathematician; Holder, who wrote on phonetics because he had experience of teaching deaf-mutes; Lord Monboddo, who combined law with anthropology and was interested in language as part of human behaviour. Then there are the poets, who discuss the sounds of the language because it is the raw material of their art, or because in translating they have come up against the differences between two tongues. Antiquarians see in English the badge of national glory in the past: and Noah Webster sees in the budding American English the sign of national glory in the future. The Quakers protest against a linguistic usage which emphasizes class division, and Thomas Sheridan believes that a common standard speech will make for social unity. Politicians like Horne Tooke and Cobbett are as revolutionary in some of their linguistic notions as in their political ones. The great philosophers like Hobbes and Locke believe that language, indistinct and misleading as it is, cannot be a perfect instrument of thought: and the lesser ones like Bishop Wilkins and James Harris suggest that it could, if only we would take more trouble.

Some statements are noteworthy in their accuracy, modernity and pungency. Wallis and Harris are convinced that the structure of English is not that of Latin—why should we be obsessed with case and inflection? Not all teachers would agree even yet. Heylin's sarcastic remarks on the ingenuity with which people misinterpret place-names need still to be borne in mind; John Wesley's attack on some kinds of pulpit voice is not yet out of date; nothing new has been added to the spelling-reform controversy; and seventeenth-century scholars are quite clear about the difference between Ancient Britons and Anglo-Saxons—which is more than can be said of many people today. And I doubt whether any one has put the case for Anglo-Saxon more vigorously than Elizabeth Elstob.

We have here a cross-section of the community, expressing opinions, theories, facts and what was believed to be fact. Not all the statements are true, but though I have now and then supplied a warning heading, I hope students will be encouraged to search out the facts for themselves in the standard histories of the language and the dictionaries. Again, I hope that the theories and opinions will serve as subject-matter for discussion groups and topics for essays. Finally I hope that the book will help to bring out the essential thing that the History of English need be no dry-as-dust subject, but can be a human, social and literary study which we should find as exciting and as vital as our ancestors so clearly believed it to be.

I should like to express my thanks to Professor L. C. Knights of Bristol, who suggested the book and has taken constant interest in the project: to Professor Dorothy Whitelock of Cambridge, Mrs Margaret 'Espinasse of Hull, Professor C. L. Wrenn of Oxford, and Professor R. M. Wilson of Sheffield, who offered constructive criticism and practical encouragement: to my colleagues Mr C. H. Gifford, whose Latin is better than mine, and Dr A. Basil Cottle, whose proof-reading is all that mine is not: to the staffs of the Bodleian Library and the Library of the University of Bristol: and not least to Miss D. Sampson for her skill and patience with the typescript. In the later stages of the book, I am grateful to the experts of the Cambridge University Press not only for its attractive appearance, but for much helpful advice about arrangement and presentation.

SUSIE I. TUCKER

THE UNIVERSITY OF BRISTOL

Note to the 1974 Edition

I wish to thank the reviewer who pointed out that besides the two examples quoted in the introduction, page 8, Verstegan was wrong in his derivation of *bough*, and *gutter*.

I wish also to thank my friend Dr. Ian Michael for drawing my attention to a wrong foot-note (p. 65). The title should be *Institutio Grammatical Puerilis (1670)*. He also pointed out that the passage from Butler is from a reprint, and that the relevant reference on p. 35. is to the chapter, not to the volume.

The title of Browne's book is wrong on the list of contents but right in the quotations.

S. I. T.

INTRODUCTION

A collection of comments on two hundred years of the mother tongue (with some notice of its relatives) offers us evidence of two kinds. The writers are historians, critics or reformers, and therefore set out both to assemble facts and to discuss them: and so they provide us with deliberately given evidence for the state of the language in their time, showing us what it was, and what in their opinion it ought to have been. But as they write, they also provide us with unconscious evidence in the things they do not mention—the usages they take for granted and illustrate in their own practice. They tell us, for example, how they pronounced particular words (by implication, correctly) and how other people pronounced them (incorrectly, of course): they list verbal forms, and tell us how to distinguish between *shall* and *will*: they explain that the difference between *thou* and *you* is conventional rather than grammatical: they notice how speech varies with the regional or social background of the speaker: and they tell us how newly-borrowed or newly-invented words sounded in the ears of those who first heard them.

Parallel with this conscious instruction runs the incidental evidence of their own way of using their language—their spelling, choice of words, sentence-structure. Camden and Verstegan in the early seventeenth century are obviously different in all three respects from the journalists and critics who contribute to the eighteenth-century periodicals, and these again differ in various subtle ways from Cobbett in the early nineteenth century. From the sentences of the seventeenth-century writers, whether loosely hung, or articulated in the Latin fashion, through eighteenth-century clarity and balance to more modern simplicity, we can trace many varieties of English style.

SPELLING

The most obvious superficial differences lie in spelling and such minor matters as the use of capitals.[1] Cobbett is quite normal to our minds, and

---

[1] The original spelling and punctuation have obvious value as linguistic evidence. Even the way capitals are used is important, if only to show that something more than a capital is needed to prove a personification. These have all been preserved: but I have not felt it necessary to ask the modern printer to reproduce the typographical practices of his predecessors, who would use italics for prefaces, quotations and proper names as well as for titles of books, illustrative words and

Horne Tooke nearly so: but, two hundred years earlier, we notice double consonants where we prefer single ones, single ones where we prefer double, *-ie* for *-y*, *y* for *i*, *-or* for *-our*, and many an additional *-e* which may or may not be historically justified: and *u* and *v* may seem to be used indiscriminately. These are differences of convention: more important is the occurrence of such correct older forms as *forraine* or *tyranne* which have not yet been burdened with their etymologically incorrect *g* and *t*.

SPELLING REFORM

The spelling-reformers have already begun their efforts to straighten things out. Camden looks back to Sir Thomas Smith's proposals, and comes to the conclusion that so many of us have come to since, when looking at later schemes—the device seems to be supported by sound and reason, but 'that Tyranne Custome' has made sure that it would never be admitted. Sir Thomas's idea that we could revive letters from the Anglo-Saxon alphabet may appeal only to phoneticians: to throw out both *c* and *q* appealed also to Ben Jonson. Both reformers were under the false impression that *k* was what the Anglo-Saxons had preferred. Neither idea has caught on—the Englishman seems to be convinced that *k* (like *z*) looks foreign except in places where he expects to see it. However, we have accepted James Howell's suggestions that we should use *y* for *ie* in such words as *pity*, and *c* for *-ck* or *-que* in such words as *public*. We might well have followed him—and Robert Bridges[1]—in reducing *some* to *som*. It is interesting to see that the Americans have followed him in the matter of *-or* for *-our*. Where fewer may serve the turn, he says, more is vain: the trouble is that we differ as to the nature of the turn to be served. Dr Johnson put the extreme opposite view when he argued that the best spelling is that which preserves the greatest number of radical letters. It is the insoluble quarrel between the phonetician and the etymologist—do we want to hear the word in our mind's ear, or do we want to see what it means—or meant, at some earlier stage of development?[2]

emphasis. Italics have been kept in the last three functions only, though I have added a note when there is any interesting use of Black-Letter, or of Anglo-Saxon or Gothic characters.

[1] Though Bridges used *som* for the unstressed form only.

[2] On the deeper problems of the word as the preserver of the past in the present, see the Preface to the 1952 edition of Owen Barfield's *Poetic Diction*.

Introduction

PRONUNCIATION

Since English spelling is so unphonetic, it is to be very gingerly handled as evidence for by-gone pronunciation. Critics discussing its insufficiency or ambiguity, or recording dialect variants, are more useful informants. Sir Thomas Smith is helpful on the quantity of vowels, and shows that the *u* in *buy* meant no more to him than it does to us: Howell explains the pronunciation of *people*, *treasure* and *Parliament* when he says they ought to be spelt *peeple*, *tresure* and *parlement*. Wallis offers evidence for the diphthongal character of *i*, which we should expect: what we do not expect, from our own habits, is the *y*-sound before front vowels and the *w*-sound before rounded ones in such words as *can* and *pot*. To him these may occur sporadically anywhere, to us they are dialectal. It is interesting to note that he feels it is careless to drop the *l* in *walk* and *talk*: many nowadays feel the same about *falcon*. His comments on how to pronounce the *o* in *London, condition* and *come* look forward to the present arguments about *comrade, combat* and *Compton*. Dyche's *Guide to the English Tongue* offers quite a number of points of contrast between what he notes or recommends and what we say over 200 years later.

Wallis and Holder are concerned with the actual phonetic principles that lie behind our pronunciation.

USAGE

Evidence on usage is three-fold: we may find support for our own habits going back further than we might have expected, or we may find ourselves watching an idiom, to which we are accustomed, struggling for acceptance: and we shall find categorical statements that such and such forms are correct, when we should call them wrong.

An example of the first is the '*shall* and *will* problem', which speakers of English outside the circle of Southern Standard are apt to regard as a mystery, a nuisance or a piece of nonsense, according to their upbringing and nationality. It is surprising to find Noah Webster upholding the distinction between these auxiliaries though he favours 'Who did he marry?' and 'You was.' Here Dr Wallis's rules, in print by 1653, still hold good.

English seems never to have had the '*tutoyer*' socio-linguistic problem as acutely as some of its neighbours, though a forgetfulness of its existence will blunt the edge of some conversations in Chaucer, 'Sir Gawayne and the Grene Knight', or Shakespearian comedy. *Thou*, says Wallis, is

3

usually contemptuous, or familiarly caressing: custom requires the plural when addressing one person, though it also requires the incorrect *you* for the older *ye* in the nominative.

At this distance it is not easy to take very seriously the Quaker onslaught against this piece of politeness. We feel, and so did George Fox's contemporaries, that it is making a moral and religious mountain out of an idiomatic mole-hill to quarrel with common usage. No doubt it is illogical—but it errs on the right side, and nowadays at least is not meant to encourage the deadliest of the Deadly Sins. Cobbett says the last word on it—'What a whole people adopts and universally practises must be deemed correct.'

As to differences of word-form, this is most noticeable in the verbs, as a glance at Lowth's *Grammar* amply demonstrates. He too concludes that we cannot fly in the face of custom—'I have gave' would shock us, but our ears have grown familiar with 'I have wrote', he says. He would be pleased to know that twentieth-century ears are as shocked at the one as at the other: and our more correct usage is also in line with Cobbett's.

VOCABULARY

Vocabulary is always shifting its ground. Usually the context is enough to explain an unfamiliar shade of meaning if we are observant enough. I have rarely felt it necessary to interpret my authorities' words, though an occasional Latinism, idiom or by-form has needed a footnote. But uses that are more free or more restricted than ours can easily be found— we should not speak of peoples being *extant*; *the fountains of Rhene* sounds poetical for *the source of the Rhine*; we prefer *improper* to *unproper*. We no longer *marvel*, in plain prose; *conceiptes* of the mind have become *concepts*; we no longer *mollify* words.

When we look at the critical comments on vocabulary, we find that some words we now accept had a rough passage. It is true that technicalities like *Pasch* or *Azimes* have not been found acceptable: but we have accepted *holocaust*, which has not ousted *burnt-offering*, but proved useful in a wider range of application, not foreseen when it was introduced. L'Estrange's odd words were reasonable targets for adverse criticism, but there is something to be said for his method of self-defence. Most critics who ventured to prophesy which new words would last have been proved wrong. We find it hard to share in Archibald Campbell's annoyance at 'great poetical powers': we all like to 'take the lead' on occasion, and we are not deterred by his objection that it is a vile phrase taken from the card- or billiard-table. Such words as *devoid, succumb, paucity, hilarity* and *repugnant* do not trouble us at all. We should pause before offering unreasoned criticism of new departures from the norm. *Youthify* in an advertisement may well strike us as shocking—but for Polonius and perhaps for his creator, *beautified* was a vile phrase too, though it doesn't worry us.

Semantic change is full of social interest: it is well illustrated here by the eighteenth-century comments on the decline and fall of *gentleman* and *genteel*.

LINGUISTIC IDEALS

Our authors were concerned to preserve the language where they felt it to be good, and to improve it where they felt it to be less good. They suggest various means to this end. The Royal Society set up ideals of clear plain writing, and might have developed into the Academy that was advocated alike by Swift and Defoe. To Swift, imperfection in language was better than change—a doubly dubious proposition. Perfection must be related to purpose—the perfection of one age may be the imperfection of another, so that both 'imperfection' and 'perfection' are relative terms. Dr Johnson declared that we could say nearly everything worth saying in the language of the days of Elizabeth I: Shakespeare himself could not carry on an ordinary conversation with the subjects of Queen Elizabeth II in his own tongue, if the talk turned to plastics or nylons, jet planes or atomic piles, nuclear fission or moon-rockets. Neither could his wife do the shopping in hers.

The implicit assumption that a language need not change is contradicted by all experience of living tongues. It is useless to point to Augustan Latin, for example, as a linguistic model at once perfect and stable; it is only an artificial abstraction cut out from the growing organism of the language.

The restrictions an Academy might wish to impose are only too clear in Defoe's proposal that no one should be allowed to use a word without approval of the committee. Can we imagine a scientist or an advertisement writer, let alone a poet, waiting for any such thing?

Another impracticable ideal is set up by the philosophers, to whom current language is vague, inaccurate and illogical. So we have Bishop Wilkins inventing a sign language, after the style of his predecessors Dalgarno and Seth Ward—a language based on strict logical categories and definitions, free from all the irregularities and insufficiencies of natural English. We should be free from the curse of Babel, he argues, if everybody could be made to agree 'upon the same way . . . of Expression as they do in the same Notion'—and the trouble is, though he does not seem to realize it, they don't even agree in the Notion. The Universal Language project is doomed to fail so long as it is based on the behaviour of one family of languages only. The Eskimo or the Hopi Indian does not think or even perceive in the patterns that the European uses, and language and thought are intricately bound up together. This, incidentally, has a bearing on the new discipline of General Linguistics and on the question of what a mechanical translating machine can be reasonably expected to do.

GRAMMAR

Wilkins and James Harris are full of interesting and provocative suggestions about philosophical grammar as against what the Bishop calls 'instituted' grammar. Other grammarians are content to collect and classify what actually happens in the language, and to lay down rules to correct faults. Lowth and Cobbett are both prescriptive and descriptive, though their explanations may not agree. Wallis is more interesting, in his insistence that English Grammar and Latin Grammar are two different things: his remarks might well be taken to heart by any modern teachers whose only conception of English grammar is that it must be taught, if at all, to prepare the way for their classical colleagues.

Noah Webster is a refreshing iconoclast, to whom the current usage in good speech is worth every technical rule ever invented.

SPEECH

English is not all words and syntax, but something we say aloud. Thomas Sheridan is the champion of spoken English, and combines his exhortations to clarity and beauty with amusing, if scathing, comments on the Irishman and the Cockney, and those who mismanage the aspirate. He envisages English as a university subject—but it is enunciation he is concerned with. Whether he would have approved of any modern syllabus we cannot tell: but he would certainly have wanted us to insist on an oral test, not to tie up loose ends in the scripts or to help the candidates over the line on the right side, but to make sure that their command of the spoken tongue is all it ought to be. So Lord Monboddo deplores the mispronunciations of his day (about which he is unduly pessimistic) and the undignified chatter he hears all round him. What would he have thought of the average broadcast 'radio family' or variety show, with its appeal depending largely on the use of sub-standard English?

ENGLISH AND ITS RELATIONS

Besides giving us a view of English as it was, and telling us how it struck contemporaries, our authorities are ready to look further afield. They are not insular. They are fascinated by the relationship of English to other languages, and it is noteworthy that the seventeenth century has a surprisingly sure historical grasp. Camden's linguistic history, like Verstegan's, is food for patriotism, but he has a correct knowledge of the Germanic group of languages and knows the story of Ambassador Busbeq who came upon the last flicker of Gothic in the Crimea. Verstegan is interested in the Latin group, incidentally, and in how French affected English after the Conquest. His anecdote of the carter in Flanders who was mistaken for an English countryman could be provided with modern parallels. The briefest holiday abroad will enable us to recall similar snatches of conversation that sounded like English—the Icelander at a picnic saying 'Villtu egg?' the Norwegian taxi-driver's 'Hvor til?' the Dutch tourist-agent's 'Kan ik U helpen?'

It is untrue that London got its name from any Continental place similarly called, as Howell would have us believe, since it had been Londinium long before the Saxon invasions: but Howell is quite clear about the relation—or lack of it—of English to the language of the ancient Britons, and he has interesting comments on the larger dialectal subdivisions of our tongue. Wallis goes further, and explains the relationship of the various Celtic languages and the preservation of them in regions where neither Roman nor Saxon had penetrated, though he underestimates the Danes. But he is sound on the Norman influence and the social and political facts behind it.

When our authorities try to get back beyond Germanic, they have inklings of Indo-European, but no real evidence. Camden knows about Scaliger's theory that Germanic is an offshoot of Persian, but he receives it with some scepticism. Monboddo thinks that Gothic is the ancestral form of Germanic; he is making the same mistake that students still make when they suppose that, because it is the oldest Germanic language recorded in a written literature, it must be the ancestor of all its sisters that did not get themselves down in writing till some centuries later. It was not possible for earlier scholars to think in our terms, for the great impetus to comparative philology came from a knowledge of Sanscrit, and that was only to be had after Sir William Jones had worked in India late in the eighteenth century. Of course Monboddo is wrong in claiming that he will be able to prove that Greek is a descendant of Sanscrit, but he is fumbling for the right key. It is entertaining to read Heylin's amused dismissal of the theory that Hebrew is the mother tongue of earth and heaven.

Latin is quoted not only to show its relation to French and its direct or indirect influence on English, but also as evidence of linguistic phenomena akin to those to be seen in English. Brerewood uses its history to show how difficult it is to abolish the native language of a populous country. He wonders whether it was ever perfectly spoken in the provinces, quoting some striking analogical 'regular' forms in use in Africa in St Augustine's time.

ANGLO-SAXON AND ITS USES

Certain specialists among our authorities look back to Anglo-Saxon with an enthusiasm compounded of patriotic feeling, historical inquiry, the grammarian's wish for explanation and the antiquary's love of old words. To illustrate this last interest, I have quoted some of Verstegan's etymologies, all of which are correct except *Brydguman* and *wynsum*, though his forms are not all impeccable. William L'Isle is determined to read Anglo-Saxon, because it will help to further his antiquarian and theological interests: why, he asks, should the technical terms of Christianity be obscured by words of Latin origin when there were better ones in Old English, that we have forgotten? The question ignores the contribution of the Latin Fathers and scholastic philosophers, and the answer is that we cannot bring back the older words now since they would be more foreign than the foreigners. But his plea for Anglo-Saxon as the vehicle of our early history and the fame of so great a man as King Alfred is as just as it is eloquent. Miss Elstob carries the argument further: her forthright comments and claims may well be read and pondered along with L'Isle's by those students who wonder why there should be a place for Anglo-Saxon in a crowded English syllabus. I have added some of George Hickes's Grammar of Anglo-Saxon to show the more technical approach. It alone would have saved later theorists such as Addison—who is here no wiser than Wallis—from the notion that *'s* is a contraction of *his*: Wallis indeed was still more absurd, when he laid it down that *his* was a miswriting of *hees*!

Some linguistic comment of a technical sort has been quoted in order to give the student a chance to test his own brains. Wallis has other errors about plurals and diminutives, which serve to show that more knowledge of Anglo-Saxon would have enlightened him. The same is true of Dr Johnson, when he writes off *length* as an irregularity compared with *long*. Much worse examples can be found among Horne Tooke's often perverse explanations. He is a stern warning that enthusiasm for language study is not of much use unless we are prepared to be accurate: Mr Bruckner deals with him faithfully. But the most enlightening example is the Chatterton controversy, especially the defence of the Rowley poems published by Dean Milles. It would be an excellent exercise for any student of Middle English to work over his arguments and examples without recourse to Tyrwhitt and show just what is wrong with them.

Cobbett is another who would have been profitably chastened by a knowledge of Anglo-Saxon. On the face of it, his assertion that 'if he make' contains an infinitive depending on an understood auxiliary—'if he [should] make'—is sensible and seems even probable, but it so happens that it can be proved from the forms of the Anglo-Saxon verb that it isn't true. Dogmatic statements about syntax, semantics and morphology are usually all the better for a little historical measurement: we bypass such knowledge at our own risk.

LANGUAGE AND SOCIETY

Our authorities are interested in the language as it is adjusted to social habit and convention. Defoe feels that clergymen, lawyers and physicians speak in a language prescribed by their professions, using a technical jargon as a matter of course: he has hard things to say about academic English. Monboddo agrees with him. Defoe is equally firm with those who cannot speak without a volley of oaths or a cascade of commonplaces. It may be doubted, however, whether such speakers could be persuaded to turn their foolish discourse into Latin to test its impropriety.

The Guardian offers us a comic skit on the man who grades his forms of address from 'My Lord, your most humble servant' to 'Hah! Frank, are you there?' according to his friends' standing. The happy-go-lucky fear of pedantry noticed by Swift is dealt with humorously in *The World* where the Editor promises to 'hang the grammar and write like a gentleman'. But where indeed do we draw the line between correctness and pedantry, between ease and carelessness?

Harris's demonstration of how the same sentiment can appear on the poetic, prosaic and slangy levels shows a useful appreciation of words as the form of thought. Affectation is laughed at wherever it is found. There are the Highwayman who claims to be a gentleman and Betty who thinks a Rout in the kitchen would be very genteel. There are, too, the overworked vogue-words: the double sense of *odd man* and *good man*: the over-use of exotic words brought in by war and commerce, and the colloquial transference of technical terms whereby we drink according to the state of our finances as if we were M.P.s speaking on the Budget. The satirical definitions of currently misused words in *The Gray's Inn Journal* are a devastating footnote to eighteenth-century society and morals.

DIALECT

Differing attitudes to local dialect were expressed then as they are now. Defoe is shocked by it—how could that Somerset schoolboy so corrupt the words of Holy Writ? It is ironic to find that *don* and *doff* which to him were countrified 'abridgements' sound to us bookish. With a truer sense of history, Sheridan calls every variety of English a dialect, though he recognizes that the one which can be acquired only by conversing with the people in polite life is, for that reason, a proof that you have kept good company: that is what its prestige depends on. He notes the embarrassment of the Irish gentleman who has observed that his vowels differ from those of his English counterpart. We may note that Sheridan calls the 'intrusive R' a cockney vice: it is now widely current, and accepted by the B.B.C. It is an odd example of time's revenges that we should throw out the *r* where it is etymologically justifiable, and then slide it in where it is not. However, we have not misplaced all the aspirates as he feared we should.

Francis Grose is frankly interested in dialect, to the extent of compiling a dictionary of that as well as one of the Vulgar Tongue—which is a collection of slang words, some of them vulgar in every sense of that double-edged word. He is aware that dialects preserve archaic native words, as well as corrupted foreign ones.

Webster draws a contrast between the many dialects in so small a country as England and the uniformity of language across the wide spaces of America. He agrees with Thomas Sheridan that such a uniformity is socially all to the good, because it unites the nation and bridges class-divisions. I suspect that both critics would be disappointed if they could come back to us now: progress in this direction has not been as rapid in this country as Sheridan hoped, and surely Webster would notice some regress in the United States.

Some words in Cooper's list of barbarous pronunciations will give us a shock: *vittles, shugar, shure, sez*—how odd they look, and the last of them illiterate. But the spelling conveys clearly the essential fact—that in the twentieth century we teach as correct what the seventeenth-century grammarians censured as wrong, or at best careless.

ARCHAISM

At the other extreme from dialect, our authorities offer some rather limited views on poetic diction. *The Guardian* is amused at such archaic patches as *Welladay, whilome* and *youngling*, and at vocabulary in general that has been picked up from glosses to Chaucer: imitation Miltonics, too, come in for its ridicule. On the other hand, Hickes is impressed by the pictorial quality of Anglo-Saxon compounds, and Bishop Percy is excited by Icelandic kennings.

METAPHOR

As to figurative language, Arthur Murphy feels that metaphor is necessary, but can be overdone: Monboddo analyses the need to express our ideas in metaphor because of lack of proper terms, which is a weakness. He notes also that metaphors borrowed at second-hand from ways of life the speaker has never experienced will inevitably be misapplied.

Harris has some funny examples of metaphors incongruously used or outrageously mixed—failures of taste still very much with us.

TONE AND TUNE

Words on the page are alive to the mind, and we can come to some idea of what they sounded like from the spelling or comments of phoneticians or grammarians if we want to hear them, not as we pronounce them, but according to the period. But can we recover all those modifications which are supplied by the tone of the voice, musical, ironical, crisp, wheedling? John Wesley must have known as well as anybody of his time how to address a crowd: he objects to every sort of affected tone of voice, whether incantatory, theatrical or over-solemn. His rules are sound: to speak in public as you do in conversation with a friend, and to vary the voice easily and naturally. Monboddo says English is defective in rhythm and melody, and there are many adverse comments on its harshness and on the vehemence of our stress-accent. Shaftesbury compares our heavy monosyllables to the hammer of a paper-mill: to Monboddo, the rhythm of English is like the beating of a drum. English monosyllables are the target of attack for many reasons: they sound ugly, they clog the smooth flow of verse, they are permanent witnesses to our careless loss of weak syllables, they are slangy abbreviations, they are Teutonic barbarisms, and quite unlike words of classical origin. Some of this is purely a matter of personal opinion, some of it is patently untrue. Anglo-Saxon is not noticeably monosyllabic, let alone Gothic or Old Norse, as a glance at Hickes's *Thesaurus* would have proved. On the other hand, Latin and French have enriched our language with monosyllables as useful and diverse as *pen* and *ink*, *pear* and *plum*, *joy* and *peace*. Aided by the native love of short-cuts, Latin itself enables us to talk of the *pros* and *cons* of the matter.

It is surprising how long this element in our speech worried the critics, and how easily they supplied rationalizations of their prejudices. Jeffreys's defence of monosyllables is a welcome oasis where a great cloud of unnecessary dust has been raised.

Some of our authorities notice how borrowed words provide evidence of the cultural relations between different countries. Harris displays our debt to the rest of Europe by referring to the languages from which they come all sorts of technical terms for the arts, from Literature to Cookery.

I have included Dryden's comment on how and why to use loan-words, easily accessible as it is, because it seems to me to be a classic defence of the process.

THE VIRTUES OF ENGLISH

On the whole, our authorities are proud of English and optimistic about its future. It is copious and yet concise, pithy and 'significative'. L'Isle praises it for conciseness: no tongue is able more shortly and with less doubtfulness to give utterance and make way for the cumbersome conceits of the mind. Addison holds it to be an enemy to loquacity, but I feel his praise is rather back-handed—he does not really approve of monosyllables and telescoped phrases. As a matter of history, most of his fears that current shortened words would be accepted have proved groundless, though we still make our own curtailments.

There is more general praise of the opposite virtue of copiousness. Cooper is impressed by our multitude of synonyms. Our borrowings from other good tongues have enriched and beautified English, according to Camden, though Wallis feels that we have an inordinate itch to borrow from abroad, so that copiousness is in danger of degenerating into luxury. Chesterfield thinks much the same, and criticism levelled at Dr Johnson made great play with his undue Latinisms, though his detractors did not as a rule use words of Latin origin with his felicitous awareness of their exact meaning.

Lowth, as a grammarian, is impressed by the simplicity of the structure and accidence of English and the difficulty of explaining what is simple. So Dr Johnson, as lexicographer, found that it is the 'simple' words that give the worst trouble—how can one define *cat*, *dog*, *rose* and keep the definition from being more complicated than the word to be defined?

Chesterfield notes with pride that English is spreading over Europe, not so much by conquest like French as by the importance and attractiveness of our literature. Webster looks forward to the twentieth century, when English in America will be spoken by 100 millions: and he is not sorry to think that with the passage of time it will be as different in the United States from British English as that is from its Continental relatives. One reason for this will be its isolation. If Webster could have had a preview of our own age as it is, he would have seen his isolation shattered by the aeroplane, the radio and the inter-continental missile: but perhaps he would have found some compensation in the influence of his language on ours. He was proud of the purity of idiom he found current in his own country: he might be more doubtful about it now, when so many languages besides English have crossed the Atlantic and added their contributions to the American amalgam.

RETROSPECT AND PROSPECT

English continues to change and expand: both processes are signs of growth. Vocabulary must keep up with modern inventiveness in everything from philosophy to packaging. In the welter of new words, and the uncertainty of new usages, it is well to look back into the history of our language. There we shall find our ancestors going through it all in their day. For them, the question was, How much Latin and Greek can we absorb? For us it is still that, with an added worry about how much American. For them it was, Shall we teach English Grammar as if it were Latin? For us it is often, Shall we teach Grammar at all? For them it was, How shall we find words for the new ideas and things that have come in with the rediscovered knowledge of the Renaissance and the new science of the seventeenth century? For us it is, How shall we name the new picture of the Universe as our scientists reveal it, and what shall we call the things that applied science puts in our hands? The purist still has to decide between common usage and historical accuracy, and when to admit that he has been plainly borne down by numbers. The poet still has to find how to express himself, and—what many seem to find harder —how to communicate his thought. Control and freedom are still at odds. Our spelling still testifies to the tension between custom and logic, between the etymological picture and the echo of the sound. We still find affectation irritating or comic: we still place a man by his accent or his choice of words. We still need to remember when we discuss the literature of the past that our first duty is to come to it humbly, acknowledging that those who wrote it knew the English language of their day better than we can ever do, and were alive to overtones that we may catch only through the hints they have left us, if at all.

If readers come away from a study of the passages in this book fortified by a knowledge of how English speakers used their language in the past, they may feel on firmer ground when confronted with the problems of the present. Awareness of differences of opinion and shifts of usage may save them from unhistorical dogmatizing, and teach them that the answer to some linguistic puzzles is not This exclusive of That, but Both, or Either, according to circumstances. I hope especially that the paragraph I have borrowed from James Harris to prefix to the whole collection will be laid to heart, and that the book may excite its readers to curiosity and inquiry into both past and present. By so doing, they will recognize the continuous organic growth of our speech from that foreign-looking language that was nevertheless called English in and before the days of King Alfred to the one written language of the modern English-speaking world. It is a unity in diversity, overriding territorial boundaries and carrying a common culture, however varied the local and temporal manifestations. This country, before the Norman Conquest, might be divided politically into Wessex, Northumbria and the rest: but the language of all the states of the Heptarchy was English in the estimation of its speakers. So today, Great Britain and the United States, Australia and Canada, and every other country with roots in Britain, call their language English. We should remember, too, that it serves as the most useful medium of communication for peoples who have no part in it by race. They may have had it imposed upon them, or have chosen it: whichever way, it serves.

And we must see that it continues to be serviceable. It is the form and expression of our emotion and our thought, of our imagination and our whole consciousness. Though we make it, it also makes us. To see that it is pure, flexible and precise, is to be concerned, not with a superficial grace, but with the essence of our civilization.

WILLIAM CAMDEN (1551-1623)

This English tongue is extracted, as the nation, from the Germans the most glorious of all now extant in Europe for their morall, and martiall virtues, and preserving the liberty entire, as also for propagating their language by happie victories in France by the Francs, and Burgundians, in this Isle by the English-Saxons, in Italy by the Heruli, West-Goths, Vandals, and Lombards, in Spaine by the Suevians and Vandales. And this tongue is of that extension at this present, that it reacheth from Suiserland, and from the fountains of Rhene over all ancient Germany both high and low as farre as the river Vistula (except Bohemia, Silesia, and part of Polonia which speake the Sclavonian tongue) and also over Denmarke, Sueden, Gotland, Norway, Island to the Hyperborean or Frozen Sea; without any great varietie, as I could prove particularly. [The conquest of France, Italy and Spain failed to supplant the 'provinciall Latine', but][1] the English-Saxon conquerours, altered the tongue which they found here wholly: so that no British words, or provinciall Latin appeared therein at the first: and in short time they spread it over this whole Island, from the Orcades to Isle of Wight, except a few barren corners in the Western parts, whereunto the reliques of the Britans and Scots retired preserving in them both their life and language. For certaine it is that the greatest and best parts, the East and South of Scotland, which cal themselves the Lawland-men, speak the English tongue varied onely in Dialect, as descended from the English-Saxons: & the Old Scottish, which is the very Irish, is used onely by them of the West, called the Hechtland-men, who call the other as the Welsh call us Sassons, Saxons both in respect of language and originall as I showed before.

I dare not yet here affirme for the antiquitie of our language, that our great-great-great grandsires tongue came out of Persia, albeit the wonderfull linguist Joseph Scaliger hath observed, *Fader, Moder, Bruder, bond*, etc. in the Persian tongue in the very sence as we now use them.

It will not be unproper I hope to this purpose, if I note out of the Epistles of that learned Ambassador Busbequius, how the inhabitants of

[1] [Summaries of shortened passages and any comments of my own are in square brackets. S.I.T.]

Taurica Chersonessus, in the uttermost part of Europe Eastward, have these words, *Winde, Silver, Korne, Salt, Fish, Son, Apple, Waggen, Singen, Ilanda, Beard,* with many other in the very same sence and signification, as they now are in use with us, whereat I marvelled not a little when I first read it. But nothing can be gathered thereby, but that the Saxons our progenitors, which planted themselves here in the West, did also to their glory place Colonies likewise there in the East.

Remaines concerning Britaine (1605)
(quoted from edition of 1637, pp. 20, 22 =
edition of 1605, p. 13, but slightly fuller).

MONOSYLLABLES

As for the Monosyllables so rife in our tongue which were not so originally, although they are vnfitting for verses and measures, yet are they most fit for expressing briefly the first conceipts of the minde, or *Intentionalia* as they call them in schooles: so that we can set downe more matter in fewer lines, than any other language. . . .

I cannot yet but confesse that we have corruptly contracted most names both of men and places, if they were of more than two sillables, and thereby hath ensued no little obscuritie.   *Ibid.* (1605), p. 21.

ENGLISH A DISGRACEFUL MIXTURE?

Whereas our tongue is mixed, it is no disgrace, when as all the tongues of Europe do participate interchangeably the one of the other, and in the learned tongues, there hath beene like borrowing one from another. As the present French is composed of Latin, German, and the old Gallique, the Italian of Latin and German-Gotish, and the Spanish of Latine, Gotish-German, and Arabique, or Morisquo. Yet it is false which Gesner affirmeth, that our tongue is the most mixt and corrupt of all other. For if it may please any to compare but the Lords Prayer in other languages, he shall finde as few Latine and borrowed forraine words in ours, as in any other whatsoever. Notwithstanding the diversitie of Nations which have swarmed hither, and the practise of the Normans, who as a monument of their Conquest, would have yoaked the English under their tongue, as they did under their command, by compelling them to teach their children in Schooles nothing but French, by setting downe their lawes in the Norman-French, and enforcing them most rigorously to pleade and to be impleaded in that tongue onely for the space of three hundred yeares, untill King Edward the third enlarged them first from that bondage. Since which time, our language hath risen by little, and the proverbe proved untrue, which so long had beene used, Jacke would be a gentleman, if he could speake any French.

Ibid. (1637), pp. 29–30 (fuller than in 1605 edition).

THE VIRTUES OF ENGLISH

Great verily was the glory of our tongue before the Norman conquest in this, that the olde English could expresse most aptly, all the conceiptes of the mind in their owne tongue without borrowing from any.

[Examples are *Leorning Cnihtas* for *disciples*: *inwit* for *conscience*: *ealdfader* for *grandfather*: *Doreward* for *Porter*.]   *Ibid.* (1605), pp. 18 ff.

The alteration and innovation in our tongue as in all others, hath beene brought in by entrance of Strangers, as Danes, Normans, and others which have swarmed hither, by trafficke, for new words as well as for new wares, have alwaies come in by the tyranne Time, which altereth all vnder heaven, by Vse, which swayeth most, and hath an absolute command in words, and by Pregnant wits: specially since that learning after long banishment, was recalled in the time of King Henry the eight, it hath beene beautified and enriched out of other good tongues, partly by enfranchising and endenizing strange words, partly by refining and mollifying olde words, partly by implanting new wordes with artificiall composition, happily containing themselves within the bounds pre-scribed by Horace. So that our tong is (and I doubt not but hath beene) as copious, pithie, and significative, as any other tongue in Europe: and I hope we are not yet and shall not heereafter come to that which Seneca saw in his time, [When mens mindes beginne once more to inure them-selues to dislike, whatsoeuer is vsuall, is disdained.][1] They affect noveltie in speech, they recall forworne and uncuth words, they forge new phrases, and that which is newest, is best liked; there is presumptuous and farre fetching of words. And some there are that thinke it a grace if their speech doe hover, and thereby hold the hearer in suspence: you know what followeth.

Omitting this, pardon me, and thinke me not overbalanced with

[1] [From the 1623 edition, where the meaning of this sentence is clearer.]

affection, if I thinke that our English tongue is (I will not say as sacred as the Hebrew, or as learned as the Greeke) but as fluent as the Latine, as courteous as the Spanish, as courtlike as the French, and as amorous as the Italian, as some Italianated amorous have confessed. Neither hath any thing detracted more from the dignitie of our tongue, than our own affection of forraine tongues, by admiring, praising, and studying them above measure: whereas the wise Romans thought no small part of their honour to consist in the honour of their language, esteeming it a dishonour to answer any forraine[1] in his owne language.

Ibid. (1605), pp. 20–1.

SOUND AND SYMBOL

Whereas the Hebrew Rabbines say, and that truly, that Nature hath given man five instruments for the pronouncing of all letters, the lips, the teeth, the tongue, the palate and throate; I will not denie but some among vs do pronounce more fully, some flatly, some broadly, and no few mincingly, offending in defect, excesse, or change of letters, which is rather to be imputed to the persons and their education, than to the language. . . .

This variety of pronuntiation hath brought in some diversitie of Orthographie, and heere-vpon Sir John Price, to the derogation of our tongue, and glorie of his Welsh, reporteth that a sentence spoken by him in English, & penned out of his mouth by foure good Secretaries, severally, for trial of our Orthography, was so set downe by them, that they all differed one from the other in many letters: whereas so many Welsh writing the same likewise in their tongue varied not in any one letter at all. Well, I will not derogate from the good Knights credite; yet it hath beene seene where tenne English writing the same sentence, have all so concurred, that among them all there hath beene no other difference, than the adding, or omitting once or twice of our silent *E*, in the end of some wordes. . . .

Sir Thomas Smith her Majesties secretary not long since, a man of great learning and iudgement, occasioned by some vncertainty of our Orthographie, though it seeme grounded vpon Sound, Reason, and Custome, laboured to reduce it to certaine heads; Seeing that whereas of Necessity there must be so many letters in every tongue, as there are simple and single sounds, that the Latine letters were not sufficient to

[1] [*forrainer* in 1637.]

expresse all our simple sounds. Therefore he wished that we should have A short, and A long, because *a* in *Man*,[1] and in *Mân* of horse hath different sounds; *E* long as in *Mên* moderate, and *e* short as in *Men*, and an English *e* as in *wée, thée, he, me, I* long, and *I* short, as in *Bi, per,* and *Bí, emere*: *O* short, and *O* long, as in *smōk* of a woman, and *smôke* of the fire: *V* long, as in *Bût, ocrea,* and *V* short, as in *Bút, Sed*: and *V* or *Y* Greeke, as *slu, nu, tru.* For consonants he would have *C* be never vsed but for *Ch,* as it was among the olde English, and *K* in all other words; for *Th,* he would have the Saxon letter Thorne, which was a *D* with a dash through the head, or *þ*; for *I* consonant the Saxon ʒ, as *ʒet,* not *Ieat* for *Ieat-stone, ʒay* for *Iay: Q,* if he were King of the A, B, C, should be putte to the horne,[2] and banished; and *Ku* in his place, as *Kuik,* not *quik, Kuarel,* not *Quarel: Z,* he would have vsed for the softer *s* or *eth,* and *es,* as *díz* for *dieth, líz* for *lies,* and the same *s* inverted for *sh,* as *Sal* for *shall, fles* for *flesh.* Thus briefly I have set you downe his devise, which albeit Sound and Reason seemed to countenance, yet that Tyranne Custome hath so confronted, that it will never be admitted.

Ibid. (1605), pp. 23–4.

RICHARD VERSTEGAN OR ROWLANDS (fl. 1565–1620)

LINGUISTIC CHANGE

But as all things vnder heauen do in length of tyme enclyne vnto alteration and varietie, so do the languages also, yea such as are not mixed with others that vnto them are strange and extrauagant, but euen within themselues do these differences grow, and encrease: the experience heerof is seen in this our now spoken-of Teutonic-toung, the high-duitsh differeth from the low, though neither do borrow from any extrauagant language: yf any in speaking or writing in any of these toungs do chance heer and there to thrust in a borrowed Latin or French woord, it is more then he needeth to do (seeing the Teutonic is moste copious) and more also then is tolerable; such bringing in of borrowed

---

[1] [The original uses Black-Letter and italics for most but not all of the examples. I have normalized.]

[2] [To be outlawed, a phrase from Scots Law more particularly, whose figurative use *O.E.D.* barely recognizes.]

woords beeing held absurd and friuolous. The Danish, Norwegian and Swedish, do again differ from these, and some litle each from other, & the Island[1] speech also: and yet none of them borrowing ought from any extrauagant language that originaly is not of that nature. This is a thing that easely may happen in so spatious a toung as this, it beeing spoken in so many different countries and regions, when wee see that in some seueral parts of England it self, both the names of things, and pronountiations of woords are somewhat different, and that among the countrey people that neuer borrow any woords out of the Latin or French, and of this different pronountiation one example in steed of many shal suffise, as this: for pronouncing according as one would say at London I would eat more cheese yf I had it the northern man saith, Ay sud eat mare cheese gin ay hadet[2] and the westerne man saith: Chud eat more cheese an chad it. Lo heer three different pronountiations in our owne countrey in one thing, heerof many the lyke examples might be alleaged.

These differēces in one same language do comōly grow among the comon people; & sometymes vpon the parents imitating the il pronountiation of their yong children, and of il pronountiation lastly ensuyeth il wryting. Other languages no doubt are subiect vnto the lyke, yea those three that are grown from the Latin, as the Italian, Spanish, and French, which to auoyd other examples may appeer in the name in Latin, of *Iacobus*; which in Italian is grown to bee *Giacomo*, in Spanish *Diego*, and in French *Iaques*.   *A Restitvtion of Decayed Intelligence*
(1605), ch. vii, pp. 194–6.

LINGUISTIC ORIGINS

The Netherland and Eastland speech draweth neerer to the old Teutonic then the High duitsh. [Marginal note, p. 196.]

Furthermore whereas it may bee obiected, that seeing there is such varietie found in the speeches of somany sundry prouinces, as do now speak the Moderne Teutonic toung, each beeing in length of tyme grown to some difference in woords and pronountiations from other, and to haue framed some woords in peculier vse to it self: how then may a man fynde out, where and which bee the woords which are in deed of the ancient and very Teutonic toung? To answere this in brief,

---

[1] [i.e. Iceland.]
[2] [The dialect sentences are in Black-letter in the text, without quotation marks.]

and at once; they are infallibly all those woords which do stil remain in generall vse throughout all the countries where any kynd of Teutonic is spoken, & those also that remain in vse in the moste parte of those prouinces, though the rest may haue left or forgotten them: for albeit as is aforesaid, euery countrey may haue some difference in it self, yet an infinit number of woords³ do remain so dispersed among all, or comon to all or the moste parte, that howsoeuer the ortography may heer and there perhaps through different pronountiation happen to bee varyed (and so of some not discerned for such as they truly bee) yet are such woords truly all one, and vndoubtedly of the first and moste ancient Teutonic-toung.

And as touching our English toung, which is more swarued from the original Teutonic then the other languages thereon also depending: this is the lesse to be marueled at, because wee are by the sea sequestred from the main continent where most it is in use. . . .¹

And not withstanding the somuch swaruing of our toung from the original, I durst for a trial of the great dependance which yet it holdeth with that which beeing issued from the same root is spoken in the continent, wryte an Epistle of chosen-out woords yet vsed among the people of sundry shyres of England, as also of the people of Westphalia, Friesland, and Flanders, and the countries lying between them, that should wel bee vnderstood both of Englishmen and Duytshmen, so great is the neerness of our vnmixed English with their yet vsed Duytsh. It is not lōg since that an Englishman trauailing by wagon in West-Flanders, and hearing the wagoner to call vnto his man and say De string is losse/ bind de string aen de wagen vast', presently vnderstood him as yf hee had said, The string is loose, bynd the string on the wagon fast'/ and weening² the follow³ [*sic*] to haue bin some English clown, spake vnto him in English.   *Ibid.* pp. 197–9.

FRENCH AND ENGLISH

[Frankish was] 'a kynd of Teutonic', [but] the Gaules now mixing themselues with the Franks, and with them becoming one nation they were cōtent to lose their ancient name of Gaules, and with them to

¹ [Verstegan illustrates from Wales and Cornwall.]
² [Edition of 1637, *deeming.*]
³ [Obs. for *fellow* says *O.E.D.* s.v. *follow.* It gives no supporting quotations, however.]

beare the name of Franch or Franchmen, and because the name of
Franch or French was now made generall, the broken Latin language
vsed of the Gaules, became within a whyle to bee called after the people
which now generallie spake it, and so caried as vntil now it doth, the
name of the French toung, and generally extinguished the ancient and
true French toung in deed, leauing notwithstanding many woords
thereof mingled with this later,[1] which therein do yet remain.

Ibid. p. 201.

The French . . . hauing left this language and entertayned another vnder
the same name, the Normannes coming afterward to setle among them,
brought with them an ancient lāguage of their own; which yf they had
stil kept, & brought into England, Englishmen and they had not seemed
so great strangers one to another, neither had they made any more
alteration in our toung then did the Danes, because it was in deed the
same language, and in effect all one with ours.[2] But they did in the tyme
of their beeing in France, proue so good schollers, that as the French
forgat their ancient Teutonic toung, and learned the language, which
the Gaules in steed of their own ancient lost language did then speak, so
they also learned the same, and lost their own, and that in the space, . . .
of one hundreth, and fiftie yeares. And now coming therewith to our
countrey, they could not conquere the English language as they did the
land, howbeit as alredy I haue noted, they much mingled and tempred
it with their French.

Ibid. p. 203.

SELECT ETYMOLOGIES AND SPECIMENS
OF NATIVE WORDS

[The Head-words are in Black-Letter.]

ABOGEN *Bowed.* Heerof a bow taketh name because it is made to bee
abogen or *bowed* when therewith we shoot, a Bowgh of a tree is also
so called, for beeing apt to bee *abogen* or *bowed*, and *bowes* at the very
first inuention of them were made of *bowghes* of trees, & so accordingly in our ancient language took that name.

---

[1] [i.e. latter, as in the 1637 edition.]

[2] [Cf. *Gunnlaugs saga Ormstungu,* ch. IX. 'Then King Æthelred, son of Edgar,
was ruling England, and was a good chieftain. . . . There was then one and the
same language in England as in Norway and Denmark: but the languages were
divided in England when William the Bastard conquered England.'
This is the opinion of a story-teller, rather than of a scholar.]

Richard Verstegan or Rowlands (*fl. 1565–1620*)

AETHRYNE We vse for this the French woord *Touche.*

AFGOD An *Idol*

AGOTEN *Poured-out*, goters otherwise gutters are accordingly so called.

ASTIEGNUNG For this after the Latin wee say *Ascension.* From *astige*, wee deryue many woords of mounting vpwards, as *stigh-ropes*, which we now pronounce *stiropes*, beeing first deuised with cords or ropes before they were made with leather and Iron fastned to it. Also *stighel*, now of vs pronounced *style*, *steghers*, now *stayers*, and the lyke.

AWARPEN, or AWURPEN *Thrown* or *cast.* We call in some partes of England, a molle, a *mouldwarp*, which is asmuch to say as a *cast-earth*, and when piancks or boords are awry wee say they cast, or they *warp.*

BEOM *A tree*, wee vse the name now for the tree when, it is squared out, calling it a *beame of timber*, whereby is meant a tree for buylding, for timbring in our old English is buylding.

BRYDGUMAN It is abreuiated of *Brydgoodman*, the goodman of the bryde.

BUHSOMNESSE or BUGHSOMNESSE *Plyablenesse* or bowsomnesse, to wit, humbly stooping or bowing downe in signe of obedience. Chaucer writes it *Buxsomnesse.*

WOD *Furious* or *Mad.* Wee yet retaine in some partes of England, the word *wodnes* for furiousnes or madnes.

WYNSUM According to our now ortography *win-some*, that is, easy to be wonne or obtayned.

Ibid. pp. 207, 208, 209, 211, 238, 239.

THE RHEIMS-DOUAI BIBLE (1609)

DIFFICULTIES OF SPECIALIZED VOCABULARY

Now for the strictnes obserued in translating some wordes, or rather the not translating of some, which is in more danger to be disliked, we doubt not but the discrete lerned reader, deeply weighing and considering the importance of sacred wordes . . . wil hold that which is here donne for reasonable and necessarie. We haue also the example of the Latin, and Greke, where some wordes are not translated, but left in Hebrew, as they were first spoken & written; which seeing they could not, or were not conuenient to be translated into Latin or Greke, how much lesse could they, or was it reason to turne them into English?

S. Augustin also yeldeth à reason, exemplifying in the wordes *Amen* and *Alleluia, for the more sacred authoritie therof* which doubtles is the cause why some *names of solemne Feastes, Sacrifices,* & other holie thinges are *reserued in sacred tongues,* Hebrew, Greke, or Latin. Againe for necessitie, English not hauing à name, or sufficient terme, we either kepe the word, as we find it, or only turne it to our English termination, because it would otherwise require manie wordes in English, to signifie one word of an other tongue. In which cases, we commonly put the explication in the margent. Briefly our Apologie is easie against English Protestantes; because they also reserue some wordes in the original tongues, not translated into English: as *Sabbath, Ephod, Pentecost, Proselyte,* and some others. The sense wherof is in dede as soone lerned, as if they were turned so nere as is possible into English. And why then may we not say . . . *Phase* or *Pasch, Azimes, Breades of Proposition, Holocaust,* and the like? rather than as Protestantes translate them: . . . *Passeouer, The feast of svvete breades, Shevv-breades, Burnt offerings*: etc. By which termes, whether they be truly translated into English or no, we wil passe ouer. Sure it is an English man is stil to seke, what they meane, as if they remained in Hebrew, or Greke.   Preface to the Rheims-Douai Bible. Printed
at Doway by Lavrence Kellam (1609).

EDWARD BREREWOOD (1565?–1613)

THE DIFFUSION AND DEVELOPMENT OF LANGUAGES

[Among the reasons for the spread of Latin—political, diplomatic, cultural—we must note that] the generall schooles, erected in sundry Cities of the Prouinces . . . (in which the Roman tongue was the ordinary and allowed speech, as is vsuall in vniuersities till this day) was no small furtherance to that language.   *Enqviries Tovching the Diversity of Langvages* . . . (1614), p. 16.

And indeede, how hard a matter it is, vtterly to abolish a vulgar language, in a populous country, where the Conquerers are in number farre inferiour to the natiue inhabitants, whatsoeuer art bee practized to bring it about, may well appeare by the vaine attempt of our Norman Conquerour: who although he compelled the English, to teach their young children in the Schooles nothing but French, and set downe all the Lawes

of the Land in French, and inforced all pleadings at the Law to be performed in that language (which custome continued till King Edward
the third his daies, who disannulled it) purposing thereby to haue
conquered the language together with the land, and to haue made all
French: yet, the number of English farre exceeding the Normans, all
was but labour lost, and obtained no further effect, then the mingling
of a few French words with the English. And euen such also was the
successe of the Franks among the Gaules, of the Gothes among the
Italians and Spanyards, and may be obserued, to be short in all such
conquests, where the Conquerors (being yet in number farre inferiour)
mingle themselues with the natiue inhabitants. So that, in those Coūtries
onely the mutation of languages hath ensued vpon conquests, where
either the ancient inhabitants haue beene destroyed or driuen forth, as
wee see in our Country to haue followed of the Saxons victories, against
the Brittains, or else at least in such sort diminished, that in number they
remained inferior, or but little superior to the Conquerors, whose reputation and authority might preuaile more then a small excesse of multitude.   *Ibid.* pp. 22–3.

And certainely much lesse can I perswade my selfe, that it [Latin] was
spoken abroad in the Prouinces perfectly. First, because it seemes vn-
possible for forraine nations, speciallie for the rude & common people,
to attaine the right pronouncing of it, who as we know doe ordinarily
much mistake the true pronouncing of their natiue language. . . .

And to conclude, it appeareth by Augustine in sundry places, that the
Roman tongue was vnperfect among the Africans (euen in the Colonies)
as pronouncing *ossum* for *os*, *floriet* for *florebit*, *dolus* for *dolor*, and such
like, insomuch that he confesseth, he was faine sometimes to vse words
that were no Latine, to the end they might vnderstand him.
                                                              Ibid. p. 29.

But . . . of the great alteration that time is wont to worke in languages,
our owne tongue may afford vs examples euident enough: wherein
since the times neere after, and about the Conquest, the change hath
beene so great, as I my selfe haue seen some euidences made in the time
of King Henrie the first, whereof I was able to vnderstand but few words.
To which purpose also, a certaine remembrance is to bee found in
Holinsheds Chronicle, in the end of the Conquerours raigne, in a Charter
giuen by him to the Citie of London.   *Ibid.* p. 44.

JAMES HOWELL (1594?–1666)

THE ENGLISH LANGUAGE

The Romans though they continued heer constantly above 300 yeers, yet could they not do as they did in France, Spain, and other Provinces, plant their Language as a mark of Conquest; but the Saxons did, coming in far greater numbers under Hengist from Holstein land in the lower circuit of Saxony, which peeple resemble the English more than any other men upon earth, so that 'tis more than probable that they came first from thence, besides ther is a town there call'd Lunden, and another place named Angles, whence it may be presum'd that they took their new denomination heer; Now the English though as Saxons (by which name the Welsh and Irish call them to this day) they and their language is ancient, yet in reference to this Island they are the modernst nation in Europe both for habitation, speech and denomination; which makes me smile at Mr Fox his error in the very front of his Epistle before the Book of Martyrs, wher he calls Constantine the first Christian Emperour, the son of Hellen an English woman, wheras she was purely British, and that ther was no such Nation upon earth called English at that time, nor above 100 yeers after, till Hengist invaded this Island and setling himself in it, the Saxons who came with him, took the appellation of *Englishmen.* Now the English speech though it be rich, copious, and significant, and that ther be divers Dictionaries of it, yet under favour, I cannot call it a regular language in regard though often attempted by som choice wits, ther could never any Grammar or exact Syntaxis be made of it; yet hath she divers subdialects, as the Western and Northern English, but her chiefest is the Scotic, which took footing beyond Tweed about the last[1] conquest; but the ancient Language of Scotland is Irish, which the mountaineers, and divers of the plain, retain to this day.

Familiar Letters, bk. II, no. LVI, 9 August 1630.
Second edition enlarged (1650).

ANCIENT LANGUAGES

It is an infallible rule to find out the mother and antient'st tongue of any Countrey, to go among those who inhabit the barren'st and most mountainous places, which are posts of security and fastnes, wherof

[1] [1650 edition reads *law*: *last* in edition of 1744.]

divers instances could be produc'd; but let the Biscayner in Spain, the Welsh in great Britain, and the Mountaineers in Epire serve the turn, who yet retain their ancient unmixt mother tongues, being extinguish'd in all the Countrey besides. *Ibid.* II [IX], 7 July 1630. [Misprinted XL.]

ENGLISH SPELLING

To the Intelligent Reader

Amongst other reasons which make the English Language of so small extent, and put strangers out of conceit to learn it, one is, That we do not pronounce as we write, which proceeds from divers superfluous Letters, that occur in many of our words, which adds to the difficulty of the Language: Therfore the Author hath taken pains to retrench such redundant, unnecessary Letters in this Work (though the Printer hath not bin so carefull as he should have bin) as amongst multitudes of other words may appear in these few, *done, some, come*: Which though wee, to whom the speech is connatural, pronounce as monosyllables, yet when strangers com to read them, they are apt to make them disillables, as *do-ne, so-me, co-me*; therefore such an *e* is superfluous.

Moreover, those words that have the Latin for their originall, the Author prefers that Orthography rather than the French, whereby divers Letters are spar'd, as *Physic, Logic, Afric*, not *Physique, Logique, Afrique; favor, honor, labor*, not *favour, honour, labour*, and very many more, as also he omits the Dutch K in most words: here you shall read *peeple*, not *peo-ple*, *tresure*, not *treasure*, *toung*, not *tongue*, etc. *Parlement*, not *Parliament, busines, witnes, sicknes*, not *businesse, witnesse, sicknesse; star, war, far*, not *starre, warre, farre*, and multitudes of such words, wherein the two last Letters may well be spar'd: Here you shall also read *pity, piety, witty*, not *piti-e, pieti-e, witti-e*, as strangers at first sight pronounce them, and abundance of such like words.

The new Academy of wits called l'Academie de beaux esprits, which the late Cardinall de Richelieu founded in Paris, is now in hand to reform the French Language in this particular, and to weed it of all superfluous Letters; which makes the Toung differ so much from the Pen, that they have expos'd themselves to this contumelious Proverb, The Frenchman doth neither pronounce as he writes, nor speak as he thinks, nor sing as he pricks.

Aristotle hath a topic Axiom, that *Frustra fit per plura, quod fieri* potest per pauciora, When fewer may serve the turn, more is vain. And as this rule holds in all things els, so it may be very well observ'd in Orthography. *Ibid.* (c. 1645), following sect. 6 of vol. II.

WILLIAM L'ISLE OF WILBURGHAM
(1569?–1637)
ESQUIRE OF THE KING'S BODY

LEARNING ANGLO-SAXON UNDER DIFFICULTIES

[A desire to read religious books in Anglo-Saxon] first stirred vp in me an earnest desire to know what learning lay hid in this old English tongue: for which I found out this vneasie way, first to acquaint my selfe a little with the Dutch both high and low; the one by originall, the other by commerce allied: then to reade a while for recreation all the old English I could finde, poetry or prose, of what matter soeuer. And diuers good bookes of this kinde I got, that were neuer yet published in print; which euer the more ancient they were, I perceiued came neerer the Saxon: But the Saxon, (as a bird, flying in the aire farther and farther, seemes lesse and lesse;) the older it was, became harder to bee vnderstood. At length I lighted on Virgil Scotished by the Reuerend Gawin Dowglas Bishop of Dunkell, and vncle to the Earle of Angus; the best translation of that Poet that euer I read: And though I found that dialect more hard than any of the former (as neerer the Saxon, because farther from the Norman) yet with the helpe of the Latine I made shift to vnderstand it, and read the booke more than once from the beginning to the end. Wherby I must confesse I got more knowledge of that I sought than by any of the other. For as at the Saxon Inuasion many of the Britans, so at the Norman many of the Saxons fled into Scotland, preseruing in that Realme vnconquered, as the line Royall, so also the language, better than the Inhabitants here, vnder conquerors law and custome, were able.

Divers Ancient Monvments in the Saxon Tongue . . . (1638).
'To the Reader', sect. 9.

William L'Isle (1569?–1637)

*A Vicar of Croydon in the time of King Ed.6;[1] to bring the people out of loue with the English Bible, then ready to come forth, read the beginning of a Latine Psalme, and said, Harke ye (beloued) how trimly this sounds in English: Dominus regnauit, irascuntur populi, qui sedet inter Cherubin, moueatur terra: The Lord hath reigned, the people wax mad, he that sitteth betweene the Cherubins, let the world wag. Though the Latine without due paraphrase doth sound little better. And euen such or worse is the translation that some haue giuen vs, who darken the Scriptures with obscure termes; as men hoping to fish the better for their owne purpose in the troubled streame. . . . But say (as Romanists doe) the Scripture in mother tongue is dangerous for error, and hard to be vnderstood of the people: shall not a man though hit his way better that knowes part of it, than hee that knowes neuer a foot?

Ibid. sect. 11.

No man lighteth a candle, and putteth it vnder a bushell. But little other doe they who keepe the world still in darknesse of a language vnknowne; and worse they who by their partiall translations and glosses, would make this light shine onely for their owne purpose; shutting and opening the same as they list, and carrying it (as it were) in a theeues or powder-traytors lanterne.

Ibid. sect. 12.

[Of the Rheims-Douai Version]: . . . no man hauing but the English tongue onely is able to vnderstand it. Witnesse their *Parasceue, of the Pasche,* their *Azimes,* their *Wine and Sicer,* their *with such Hosts God is promerited,* their *Supererogate,* their *Supersubstantiall bread,* and many the like.

[The Anglo-Saxon] hath words for Trinity, Vnity, Deity and Persons thereof; . . . Yea for Incarnation, for Ascension, Descension, Resurrection, for Catholike and all such forraine words as we are now faine to vse, because we haue forgot better of our owne. I speake not to haue them recalled into vse, now these are well knowne; sith I vse them and the like my selfe for the same reason; but to giue our tongue her due commendations, to shew the wilfull and purposed obscurity of those

---

* A witty Priest in my aged friends hearing, who told it me.

[1] [I have made the text into a footnote, and a marginal note into the text, in the first words of the first sentence.]

other translators, and to stop the base and beggerly course of borrowing when we need not.

For what tongue is able more shortly and with lesse doubtfulnesse, to giue vtterance and make way for the cumbersome conceits of our minde, than ours? What more plentifull, than ours might be, if we did vse well but our owne garbes, and the words and speeches of our sundry shires and countries in this Iland?   *Ibid.* sect. 16.

IN PRAISE OF ANGLO-SAXON

We lacke but a Grammar which our Saxon Ancestors neglected not, as appeares by that of this Ælfricus yet extant in many faire-written copies: ... [Anglo-Saxon is necessary for us to] come to the vnderstanding of these so venerable handwritings and monuments of our owne antiquity: without which we can neither know well our lawes nor our Histories, nor our owne names, nor the names of places and bound-markes of our Country. . . .   *Ibid.* sect. 17.

[A knowledge of Anglo-Saxon will show
  (1) that our Saxon ancestors had the Scripture and other books of Divinity in the mother tongue;
  (2) the etymologies and roots of words and names, which will prevent misunderstandings and theories based on false etymology such as the notion that Creklade implies a place where Greek was taught;
  (3) the right meaning of old laws;
  (4) the right meaning of charters, territories and place-names, etc.]
I haue found some good vse hereof in my owne grounds, and giuen satisfaction also vnto others, concerning places farre off and vnknowne to me: insomuch as the parties haue told me, that if I had knowne the country as well as themselues, I could not haue described it more rightly then I did, by the meere notation of the name thereof. This proues also that our Saxon Ancestors were a very wise and vnderstanding people, and had a very significant and composable tongue; and that they did not, as men doe now adaies, for a glory of short continuance, name the places of their conquest after themselues, or some of their great masters: but euen according to natures selfe. . . .
  . . . our language is improued aboue all others now spoken by any

nation, and became the fairest, the nimblest, the fullest. . . . Tell me not
it is a mingle-mangle; for so are all. . . .   *Ibid.* sect. 19.

[L'Isle translates a passage from Ælfric's *De veteri testamento* in which he
imagines King Alfred asking why his work for religion and education
should be forgotten:]
    Haue I translated with my owne hand the godly Pastoral of Saint
Gregory, with many his learned Homilies; yea the whole Bible it selfe;
haue I sent copies of them all to my Churches, with many Mancusses
of gold, for the helpe and incouragement of my Pastors, and instruction
of my people; that all should be lost, all forgot, all grow out of knowledge and remembrance? that my English in England, neede to be
Englished; and my translation translated; while few now, and shortly
perhaps none, shall be able to doe it? What negligence, what ingratitude
is this?   *Ibid.* sect. 20.

SIR THOMAS BROWNE (1605–1682)

LATIN VERSUS ENGLISH

Our first intentions considering the common interest of Truth, resolved
to propose it unto the Latine republique and equal judges of Europe,
but owing in the first place this service unto our Country, and therein
especially unto its ingenuous Gentry, we have declared our self in a
language best conceived. Although I confess the quality of the Subject
will sometimes carry us into expressions beyond meer English appre-
hensions. And indeed, if elegancy still proceedeth, and English Pens
maintain that stream, we have of late observed to flow from many; we
shall within few years be fain to learn Latine to understand English, and
a work will prove of equal facility in either. Nor have we addressed
our Pen or Stile unto the people, (whom Books do not redress, and are
this way incapable of reduction) but unto the knowing and leading part
of Learning.   Preface to *Pseudodoxia Epidemica* (1646)
                      (quoted from the sixth edition, 1672).

33

THE ORIGIN OF LANGUAGE

[In order to prove which nation was oldest, the Egyptian King Psammitichus] attempted this decision by a new and unknown experiment, bringing up two Infants with Goats, and where they never heard the voice of man; concluding that to be the ancientest Nation, whose language they should first deliver. But herein he forgot that speech was by instruction not instinct, by imitation, not by nature, that men do speak in some kind but like Parrets, and as they are instructed, that is, in simple terms and words expressing the open notions of things; which the second act of Reason compoundeth into propositions, and the last into Syllogisms and Forms of ratiocination. *Ibid.* bk. VI, ch. I.

JOHN WALLIS (1616–1703)

THE LANGUAGES OF GREAT BRITAIN

The English Language, . . . which is nowadays spoken not only throughout England but also used in Scotland, is not the ancient British Language which the first Britons once used, nor indeed is it an offshoot of it, but brought entirely from elsewhere.

The languages and manners were the same [on both sides of the Channel, whether because of emigration, commerce, or owing to Britain and France having once been joined by an isthmus]. Wales and Gaul have a name in common. For there is a very frequent interchange of G and W—cf. *guerre, garant, gard, gardien, garderobe, guise, guile, gage, guichet, guimblet, guerdon, Guillaum, gaigner, gaster, guetter,* etc., and *warre, warrant, ward, warden, wardrobe, wise, wile, wager, wicket, wimble, reward, William,* to *winne,*[1] to *wast,* to *wait,* etc. . . . [The language in Britain, being further removed from Rome, was less affected by Latin than the speech of Gaul, Spain or Lombardy, but many words were intermingled and retained, but made to conform to the rules of the native British speech. After the Anglo-Saxons had driven out the Britons, the language was retained in mountainous regions such as Wales, Cornwall, the Highlands of Scotland—and in Ireland, where neither Romans nor Anglo-Saxons penetrated.]

The Anglo-Saxons, having obtained the ancient seats of the Britons,

[1] [An unlucky example. I have not modernized the spelling of Wallis's English words.]

John Wallis (1616–1703)

called that part of Britain which they had gained, England, and the language they brought with them, English; which now we call Saxon or Anglo-Saxon commonly, to distinguish it from present-day English. But the language of the Anglo-Saxons was an offshoot of ancient Teutonic, related to Frankish, modern German, Dutch, Danish, Swedish and other kindred languages. It remained nearly pure in England up to the time of the Normans, though there was some give and take with Welsh. No change in the language followed the coming of the Danes, because their language was almost the same or at least closely related. When Duke William of Normandy, called the Conqueror, brought his Normans here and won England, he attempted to change English, wishing to introduce the French he used in Normandy. For though the Normans were once a Norwegian people using the same language as the Anglo-Saxons, they had changed their native tongue for French. . . . Therefore William took care that public and judicial statements should be in French. But he did not succeed, for the Normans were comparatively few, and it was easier for them to lose their tongue than to alter English. But many French words of Latin origin . . . crept into English and many English words gradually went out of use.

And since that time there has been a more than sufficient medley of exotic words. Not because the English tongue is barren of itself and deficient in words, for it is abundantly full of words . . . if you will, copious to the point of luxuriousness, nor is it short of anything in its own supplies for the complete expression of the most exact meanings, as is clear from the poetry of Spenser, whose phrasing is polished enough and elegantly adorned, and copious, but chaste and very little polluted with exotic decorations. But partly owing to various dealings abroad, and frequent intermarriages among Royalty, partly owing to too much love of innovations (especially in this last century), we have sought out foreign words with such an inordinate itch, that no one considers that anything can be said elegantly or emphatically if it does not savour of the unusual or foreign. Such a change could hardly be avoided.

And partly by these mixtures, partly by the longer passage of time, which is in the habit of making noticeable changes in other tongues, it has come about that Anglo-Saxon has been gradually changed into the present English tongue.

Grammatica Linguae Anglicanae (Oxford, 1653). (Translated from the *Praefatio ad Lectorem* with some omissions and a summary of matter within the square brackets.)

ON GRAMMARIANS

I am not ignorant of the fact that others before me have attempted to produce a Grammar of English and have not merited contempt, especially Dr Gill in Latin, Benjamin Johnson [*sic*][1] in English.... But none of them, in my opinion, proceeded on the way which is most suitable to the undertaking; for all of them have forced our tongue too much into the pattern of Latin (an error shared by nearly all teachers of other modern languages) and so have taught many useless things about the cases of Nouns, Genders and Declensions, and about the Tenses, Moods, and Conjugations of Verbs, about the government of nouns and verbs, etc., matters absolutely foreign to our language, producing confusion and obscurity rather than serving as explanations.

A new method seems necessary, one not so much adapted to Latin as to the logic of our own tongue....

Even in Latin there are some nouns and adjectives such as ... *instar, sat, frugi, nequam, præsto*, etc., which are quite indeclinable and which are supposed to have cases and genders on the analogy of other words, but which remain absolutely invariable: if all Nouns and Adjectives had been so, it is more than certain that there would have been a deep silence about cases and genders and a good deal of the syntax of the Noun would never be heeded. And so with the Moods and Tenses of the Verb if they were expressed by circumlocutions.... Why should we introduce a fictitious and quite foolish collection of Cases, Genders, Moods and Tenses, without any need, and for which there is no reason in the basis of the language itself?

Ibid. from the *Praefatio*.

SOUND AND SYMBOL

[Wallis proceeds to a discussion of how sounds are formed, giving descriptions of the vowels and consonants and a comparison of them with the sounds of other languages. For example:]

If the breath, expelled through the throat at the lips, is intercepted by closed lips, the letter *P* is formed.... If it does not reach the lips, but is intercepted in the palatal region (the tip of the tongue being moved to the front part of the palate, or, which is the same thing, to the roots of the upper teeth), the consonant *T* is formed. [He recognizes the difference between [N] and [ŋ]—in *hand* and *hang*, *band* and *bank*.

[1] [A common spelling, though 'Jonson' seems to be what its owner preferred.]

Distinguishing between *F* and *V* he says of *V*:] The Anglo-Saxons either did not have the sound [*v*] or wrote it with *f*, for they did not know consonantal *v*. They commonly wrote with *f* (as did the English for some centuries) words that are now written with *v* no less than those now written with *f*: as *gif, heofon*, etc. which are now written *give, heaven*, etc.

The Anglo-Saxons formerly used to write *θ* with the character *þ* which they called thorn 'Spina' . . . [and had a separate character for the voiced sound, but . . .] the English in following centuries used *þ* for both sounds: it gradually degenerated into *y*, which frequently appears in words now written with *th*; the habit is so strong, that even now it is not infrequently kept—y^e, y^t, y^u, for *the, that, thou*, etc.

[He points out the difference between the *th* in Chatham, the *sh* in Masham, etc. and the single sounds now rendered phonetically with [*θ*] and [*ʃ*].]

I believe the sound *Gh* to have been pronounced by the English in the words *light, night, right, daughter*, etc: but nowadays, though the spelling remains, the sound is practically entirely omitted: Northerners, especially Scots, usually keep it, or rather substitute *h* for it. The Irish have it exactly in *logh*. . . . The Germans use *ch* in words that have *gh* in English—for their *Nacht, recht, leicht, fechten, tochter*, correspond to our *night, right, light, fight, daughter*, etc: there are not a few like this.

[He notes that the substitution of *z* for *gh* in these words is a scandalous error.]

When *y* was vocalic, it was written by the Anglo-Saxons and the English who followed them with a dot over it thus, *ẏ*.

Ibid. from *De Loquela, sive De sonorum Formatione,*
Tractatus Grammaticus-Physicus, sect. III.

PRONUNCIATION

English *ī* . . . is clearly a compound of *e* feminine and *y* consonant: it is entirely the same sound as Greek ϵι. Orchard, riches sound like *ortyard, rityes*. English *wh* is always pronounced like *hw*. The Anglo-Saxons used to put the letter *h* first (why the English later put it last, I simply do not know): so for their [hpæt, hpilc] the English say *what, which*, but the Scots *quhat, quilk*.

Many put *y* before narrow vowels—*can, get, begin*, sound as if written *cyan, gyet, begyin* . . . and sometimes *w* is added to labial consonants, especially with open *o* as in *pot, boy, boile* which sound like *pwot, bwoy, bwoile,* but not always or by everybody.

The English move their enunciation forward, as it were, towards the front of the mouth, and speak with open throat: hence the greater distinctness of their sounds.

German is more guttural and French more palatal.

Ibid. De Loquela, sect. IV: *De sonis compositis.*

... *publique* is a French spelling rather than an English [he prefers *publike* or *publick*].

T before *i,* followed by another vowel, sounds like hissing *s.* This is chiefly in words of Latin descent, though not only in them—so *nation, potion, meditation, exspatiate,* etc., sound like *nasion, posion, meditasion, exspasiate,* etc. ... But after *s* or *x, t* has its genuine sound, as in *question, mixtion.* Y is usual at the end of words, but *i* more often medially.

In some words *u* or *h* (as with the French) is added to indicate the sound of *g,* as in *guift, guide, guile* ... *ghesse, Guilbert, Guifford* ... in which *u* is silent, as it is in *buy* and *build.*

Ibid. cap. I, i.

... *walk, talk* are pronounced by the more careless speakers as wauk, tauk.

Final *e* [apart from foreign words and such words as *he, the*] is quite silent. [Wallis realizes that it was once sounded as an obscure sound, many present-day monosyllables having been once dissyllabic. He notes its presence in the spelling of many words that now omit it. Why should it be there if it was not pronounced?] For it is quite useless to indicate the prolongation of a syllable, which is its chief modern use. The more accurate printers omit the *e* when there is no reason for it, though it is mostly kept after *l* as in *candle, handle* ... in which it serves no purpose and could be omitted without inconvenience. But it could be kept in *idle, trifle* ... *table, noble,* etc. to show the length of the preceding vowel. Indeed, *child, wild, mild,* etc. could be more correctly written with final *e.* [The more careless pronounce *cundition, Lundun, cumpasse;* and *come, done, some* are usually so pronounced. The sound could be spelt with a grave accent on the *o.*]

Ibid. ii.

[*Ea* nowadays is pronounced long *é.*
Ee is French *i* lengthened.
Some pronounce *tòil, òil* as *tŭyl, ŭyl.*]

Ibid. iii.

38

John Wallis (1616–1703)

cough, tough, rough, laugh, are pronounced *coff, tuff, ruff, laff*. *Inough* (singular) is pronounced *inuff*: but *inough* (plural) *enow*.   *Ibid.* iv.

[Wallis has been considering pure and genuine English, and does not think it worth while to mention regional dialects, affected female foolishness, or barbarisms, or the careless pronunciations of the common people or of courtiers or fops.]   *Ibid.*

I should not wish you to expect that everything in our Language should correspond exactly to Latin. For in this as in nearly all modern tongues, there is a great difference from the syntax of Greek and Latin (arising mainly because we do not recognize differences of cases). The few who do pay attention to them undertake more labour than the subject is worth.

Ibid. cap. II.

NOTES ON USAGE

Chicken is the plural of *chick*, and those who say *chicken* in the singular and *chickens* in the plural, are quite wrong. Also, a *fere*, plural *fern*: but many say *fern* for both numbers, but there is a plural *ferns*; for *fere* and *feres* are nearly obsolete. Some say, more rarely, *housen, eyn, shoon,* etc. for *houses, eyes, shooes,* etc. Some say a *pease,* plural *peasen*; but better, singular a *pea,* plural *peas.*

[He thinks *men, cow, swine* to be contractions of *manen, cowin, sowin.*]

Ibid.

. . . the word *his,* and the interrogative *whose* stand for *hee's, who's* . . . Some say *hern, ourn, yourn, hisn,* for *hers, ours,* etc. but it is barbarous and I do not believe anybody writes them. . . . It is to be noted that it is the custom with us (as with the French, and others nowadays) to use the plural when addressing one person, though we say *you,* not *yee.* If the singular is used it is usually contemptuous or familiar and caressing.

Ibid. cap. VII.

Do and *did* indicate present and past tense emphatically. . . .
    Shall and *will* indicate the Future.
    . . . It is difficult for foreigners to know when to use *shall* and when to use *will,* for we do not use them promiscuously. . . .
    In the 1st Person, *shall* is the simple future: *will* promises or threatens.
In the 2nd and 3rd persons, *shall* promises or threatens, *will* is the simple future.   *Ibid.* cap. IX.

PETER HEYLIN (1600–1662)

A PARODY OF THE STYLE OF HAMON L'ESTRANGE[1]

Now the Thunder-Thumping Jove transfund his Dotes into the Pericranion of our learned Author, who seems like Rhombus in Sir Philip . . . to be even gravidated with Child untill he hath endoctrinated our Plumbeus Cerebrosities, in the adæquate sence, and perceptibility of the word *Stylus*. . . .

Extraneus Vapulans, 'by a Well-willer to the Author of the
*Observations on the History of the Reign of
King Charles*' (1656), ch. II, pp. 37–8.

PLACE-NAMES

Fol. 19. [i.e. fol. 19 in Fuller's *Church History of Britain*, from which Heylin then quotes]: This relation is favoured by the name of Litchfield, which in the British tongue signifies a Golgotha, or a place bestrewed with skuls.

It's true indeed that *Litchfield*, or *Licidfield*, as Beda calleth it, is made by John Rosse to signifie *Cadaverum Campus*, or the field of dead bodies.[2] But that it doth so signifie in the British language I do more then doubt, the termination of the word being meerly *Saxon*, as in *Hefenfield, Cockfield, Campsfield*, and many others. As little am I satisfied in the Etymon of the name of *Maiden-head*, which he ascribes unto the worshipping of the head of one of those many Maidens which were martyred with Ursula at Colen. . . . For which though he cite Camden for his Author (following therein, but not approving the old Tradition) yet when I finde in the same Camden, that this Town was formerly called *Maidenhith*, that anciently there was a ferry near the place where the town now stands, and that *Hith* in the old Saxon tongue, did signifie a Wharfe, Haven, or landing place, I have some reason to believe, that the Town took this name from the Wharfe or Ferry belonging at that time to some neighbouring Nunnery, or to some private Maidens dwelling thereabout, who then received the profits of it.[3] . . .

[1] [See p. 42 for Hamon L'Estrange.]

[2] [Cf. Dr Johnson in his Dictionary, s.v. *Lich: Lichfield*, the field of the dead, a city in Staffordshire, so named from martyred Christians. For the facts, see Ekwall, *The Oxford Dictionary of English Place-names*.]

[3] [He compares Queenhith in London and Maiden Bradley in Wilts.]

Peter Heylin (1600–1662)

But to return again to *Leitch-field*, It must needs seem as strange to my judicious Reader, that one part of it should be borrowed from the Britans, and the other from the Saxons; as it seems strange unto our Author, and that justly too, that Cern in Dorcetshire should anciently be called Cernel, from the Latine word *Cerno*, which signifies to see, and the Hebrew word *El* signifying God. . . .

Examen Historicum, 'Animadversions on the *Church History of Britain*'
(by Thomas Fuller) (1659), pp. 19–20.

LANGUAGE AND SOCIETY

Fol. 15. Thus the Italian, Spanish, and French, Daughters or Neeces to the Latine, are generated from the corruption thereof.[1]

This is . . . the common and received opinion. . . . [But] it is affirmed with better reason by our learned Brerewood, That those tongues have not sprung from the corruption of the Latine, by the inundation and mixture of Barbarous people in those Provinces, but from the first imperfect impression and receiving of it in those forein Countries. For the Latine tongue was never so generally received in any of the conquered Provinces out of Italy, as to be spoken ordinarily by the common people; the Gentry and Nobility might be perfect in it, for the better dispatch of their Affairs with the Roman Magistrates. . . . And some taste of it might be found with the vulgar also, who having continual intercourse with the Roman Souldiers, and some recourse for Trade to the Roman Colonies could not but get a smattering of the Latine tongue. Just so the Gentry and Nobility both in Wales and Ireland, are trained up for the same reasons in the English tongue; which not withstanding could never get the mastery of the natural Language, or gain much ground on those of inferior quality. *Ibid. p. 36.*

WAS HEBREW THE ORIGINAL TONGUE?

The Hebrew the common Tongue of the whole world before it was inclos'd (that is to say, divided) into several Languages.[2]

An Opinion as common as the other, and as weakly grounded. . . . Nor is it the opinion only, that this Tongue was spoken universally

---

[1] [Again, the quotation is from Fuller, whom Heylin is criticizing.]

[2] [Quotation from Fuller.]

before the Flood, and even in Paradise it self in the state of innocency; but that it shall be spoken in the Celestial Paradise, the language of the Saints in glory: in somuch that some good women of my old acquaintance, were once very eagerly bent to learn this Language, for fear (as I conceive) they should not chat it handsomely when they came to heaven.

Ibid. p. 37.

HAMON L'ESTRANGE (1605–1660)

EXAMPLES OF L'ESTRANGE'S DICTION

What oblique Descants will come traverse upon this honest Narrative, I already prejudicate.

accrimination . . . enormitans (noun) . . . the vale of rural recesse . . . repandous and embowed . . . postlimineated and restored . . . extimulated and whetted . . . the respiration of auricular contrition . . . God is accostable by inorganicall and inaudible ejaculations . . . ferocient and impetuous . . . magnetique and attractive . . . radix and ground of this contest . . . clientelaries and vassalls . . . grison and step . . . to delay and superannuate this expectation . . . configurating and complying . . . exorated or be prevailed with . . . temerated and infringed . . . [Episcopacy is a] chip of the old block . . . Popery . . . from old records progs and bolts out an ancient Precedent . . . gives them the slip . . . the improsperity of that enterprise made France too hot for her. . . . But old Sir John Savill found a trick worth two of that.　*The Reign of King Charles* (1655)
(from the second edition, 1656).

L'ESTRANGE'S DEFENCE OF HIS DICTION

First, I was confident that amongst learned men they needed no other passe then their own extraction. And for those who were meer English readers I saw no reason they should wonder at them, considering that for their satisfaction, I had sent along with every forreigner his interpreter to serve instead of a Dictionary.

Then I had observed that our language had of late already admitted very neer all of them into so frequent use in ordinary discourse, as almost amounted to a Naturalization of them amongst us.

The Observator Observed: or Animadversions upon the Observations
on the History of King Charles (1656), p. 2.

WILLIAM WALKER (1623–1684)

'THOU' AND 'YOU'[1]

In the using of *you* to one, as well as to more than one (which is the Language of the Nation, not only spoken by the private persons, but extant in the both private and publick Writings of it) we do seem to imitate the French, who, as they have one word, viz. *tu* for *thou*, and one, viz. *vos* for *ye*; so they have one which they use both to one, and to more than one indifferently; namely, *vous*, *you*. Nor is this the only word which we apply to one, and to more than one. For the Pronouns *who* and *which* are so used; yea, and the nouns *swine* and *sheep*, etc. . . . Nor is this the peculiar irregularity of the English or French; the same may be found in Latin; for *qui* and *quae*, *sui*, *sibi*, and *se*, are applied indifferently to one or more. And even *nos* and *vos*, though rarely, yet may be found spoken of one as well as of more than one. . . .

As the Primitive *you*, so the Derivative *your*, is directed to one person in the publick, as well as private Writings and Speakings of the people of this land: whose custom so to speak is sufficient to make that speaking good, that which gives Authority to Words being Use; Quem penes arbitrium est, & jus & norma loquendi, as Horace saith. . . .

Notwithstanding though speaking to private persons, we say *your* indifferently to one or more, yet in Latin we observe the distinction of *tuus* to one, and of *vester* to more than one. But again, when we speak to publick Persons, as Kings, etc. then in Latin (as well as in English) we say either *tuus* or *vester*. The use of *tuus* is so far from being questioned, that it is passionately contended for by some, who reject and condemn the use of *vester* to such persons. And for the use of *vester* it is justifiable by good example. . . .

         A Treatise of English Particles, ch. 105
(quoted from the eleventh edition,[2] London, 1695).

[1] [The original is printed in a mixture of types, Roman, Italic and Black-Letter.]
[2] [The first edition is given as 1663 in the Cambridge Bibliography of English Literature, but there is a copy dated 1655 in the Bodleian Library. That of 1695 is fuller.]

GEORGE FOX (1624–1691) AND OTHERS

THE GRAMMATICAL AND SOCIAL USES OF
'THOU' AND 'YOU'

For all you Doctors, Teachers, Schollars, and School-masters, that teach people in your Hebrew, Greek, Latine, and English Grammars, Plural and Singular; that is, *Thou* to one, and *You* to many, and when they learn it, they must not practice it: what good doth your teaching do them? for he is a Novice, and an Ideot, and a fool called by *You*, that practises it; Plural, *You* to many; and Singular, *Thou* to one.

Now People, What good doth all your giving money to these School-masters, Teachers, and Doctors, to teach your children Singular and Plural, in their Accidence, and Grammars? what good doth your learning do them, when you do not intend that they should practice it, when they have learned it; that is, *Thou* to one, and *You* to many, he is called clownish, and unmannerly, if your childe practice that which he hath learned at School, which you have paid for, he is called a Clown, and unmannerly, and ill bred. . . .

But, why do the Translators translate the Bible, *Thou* to one, and *You* to many, Italian, Greek, Hebrew, and Latine; (Dutch Bibles, high and lowe) French Bibles, and Welch and English Bibles, and others, Plural and Singular, *thou* to one, and *you* to many, if the people should not practice it, *thou* to one, and *you* to many? . . .

The Teachers of the world, and Schollars have been either very Ignorant of Tongues, or else wilfull, that they would have *you* spoken to one, which is *thou*; and this may give all people to see, in saying that it was *you* in other Tongues to one, that they are them which corrupts the Languages, and are exalted, taking glory to themselves, and have the Plural put upon them, for the singular, which is vulgar.

A Battle-Door for Teachers and Professors to Learn Singular and Plural; You to Many and Thou to One: Singular One, Thou; Plural Many, You (London, 1660). From the Introduction.

PRECEPT AND PRACTICE

Now if ye say they were wise men that translated the Bible, and not fools, and Idiots, and Novices, and that the Bible is translated true . . . then ye must acknowledge your selves to be fools, and Idiots, and

Novices, and through your pride and ambition, have degenerated from your own Mother tongue English, and cannot speak proper Language plural, and singular, *thou* to one, and *you* to many, but you would have *you* to one. . . .

Then must the Schollars, and Doctors, and the raging Professors acknowledge themselves to be Novices, fools, and Idiots which they put upon them that have spoken, and do speak *thou* to one, and *you* to many, the Elect People of God, which ye in scorn call Quakers. [High and Low Dutch and French are equally degenerate, as a comparison with Latin, Greek and Hebrew, shows. In using these languages, children would be punished for using plural for singular.]

But if they practice it in their speech, they grin at them like Dogs, and fret and rage like mad men, & say What? thou's thou me ill-bred clown? I will be you'd, though it be contrary to what I have taught, or what I have been taught at School; or though it be contrary to Scripture Example, yet I will have it, because it is my will; I will follow the Roman Empires Example, the Popes, who first brought it up, *you* to one; I will not heed Scripture nor Grammar; rather than I will offend my own will, and my own proud mind, and other mens pride, who cannot bear it, I will rather deny Grammar and Scripture, and Sense and Reason: I will follow the customes of the Nations, who sayes, *you* to one and *you* to many; and so have lost distinction, though it be otherwise in the Bible and Grammars, and though it have been otherwise in former years before the Apostacy, yet let me joyn with the Pope, and his power, that first brought it in.

[The historical statement is supported by a quotation from James Howell's Epistle annexed to Cotgrave's French-English Dictionary, which follows:]

Furthermore, I find in the French language, that the same fate hath attended some words, as usually attend men, among whom we find some use to rise to preferment, others to fall to decay, and an undervalue. I will instance in a few, this word *Maistre, Master,* was a word of high esteem in former times among the French, and appliable to Noble men, and other in some high Office onely, but now it is fallen from the Baron to the Boor, from the Count to the Cobler, or any other mean Artisan, as Maistre Jean le sauuetier, Mr. John the Cobler; Maistre Jaques le Cabaretier, Mr. Jammy the Tap-house man; *Sire* was also appropriate onely to the King, but now adding a name after it is a title applyable to any mean man upon the endorsement of a letter, or other-

E 45

wise; but this word *Souuerain* clean contrary hath raised it self to that cumble of greatness, that it is now applied onely to the King, whereas in times past the President of any petty Court, any Bailiff or Seneschall was called *Souuerain*; *Mareshal*[1] likewise at first was the name of a Smith, Farrier or one that dressed horses, but it climbed by degrees, to that height that the Chiefest Commanders of the Gendarmery of France, are com'd to be called Marshalls. . . . This title *Majesty* hath no great Antiquity in France, for it began in Henry the Seconds time. And indeed it was the Stile of France at first, as well as any other Countries *Tutoyer to thou* any person one spoke unto; But when the Common wealth of Rome turned to an Empire, and so much Power came unto one mans hand, then in regard he was able to Conferr Honor and Offices, the Countries began to magnifie him, and to speak to him in the Plural Number by *You*, and to deify him with Transcending Titles . . . so that *you* in the Plural Number, with other Titles and Complements, seems to have its first rise with Monarchy, which descended afterwards by degrees upon particular men.   *Ibid.* sect. 8.

JOSEPH GLANVILL (1636–1680)

DIFFICULTIES OF DEFINITION

[The Principles of Peripatetic and Scholastic Philosophy] are steril, unsatisfying Verbosities': [a fact which] cannot escape the notice of the most shallow inquirer. . . . Only to give an hint more of this verbal emptiness; a short view of a *definition* or two will be current evidence: which, though in Greek or Latine they amuse[2] us, yet a *vernacular translation* unmasks them; and if we make them speak English, the cheat is transparent. Light is ἐνέργεια τοῦ διαφανοῦς, saith that Philosophy: In English, the *Act of a perspicuous body*. Sure Aristotle here transgrest his *Topicks*: and if this definition be clearer, and more known than the thing defin'd; midnight may vye for conspicuity with noon. Is not *light* more known then this insignificant[3] *Energie*? And what's a *diaphanous* body, but the *Lights medium*, the *Air*? So that *light* is the act of the *Air*: which definition spoils the Riddle; and makes it no wonder, a man should see by *night* as well as by *day*. . . .

The Philosopher that prov'd motion by walking, did in that action

---

[1] [Catch-word with -*ll*.]   [2] [=bewilder.]   [3] [=meaningless.]

Joseph Glanvill (1636–1680)

better define it; And that puzled Candidate, who being ask'd what a *circle* was, describ'd it by the rotation of his hand; gave an account more satisfying. In some things we must indeed give an allowance for words of Art: But in defining obvious appearances, we are to use what is most plain and easie; that the mind be not misled by Amphibologies, or ill conceived notions, into fallacious deductions.

The Vanity of Dogmatizing (1661), ch. XVI.

JOHN WILKINS (1614–1672)

WHY LANGUAGES CHANGE AND BECOME CORRUPT

Besides the common fate and corruption to which Languages as well as other humane things are subject, there are many other particular causes which may occasion such a change: The mixture with other Nations in Commerce; Marriages in Regal Families, which doth usually bring some common words into a Court fashion; that affectation incident to some eminent men in all ages, of coining new words, and altering the common forms of speech, for greater elegance; the necessity of making other words, according as new things and inventions are discovered. Besides, the Laws of forein Conquests usually extend to Letters and Speech as well as Territories; the Victor commonly endeavouring to propagate his own Language as farre as his Dominions; which is the reason why the Greek and Latin are so universally known. And when a Nation is overspread with several Colonies of foreiners, though this do not alwaies prevail to abolish the former Language, yet if they make any long abode, this must needs make such a considerable change and mixture of speech as will very much alter it from its original Purity.

Those learned Languages which have now ceased to be vulgar,[1] and remain onely in Books, by which the purity of them is regulated, may, whilst those Books are extant and studied, continue the same without change. But all Languages that are vulgar, as those learned ones formerly were, are upon the fore-mentioned occasions, subject to so many alterations, that in tract of time they will appear to be quite another thing than what they were at first.

An Essay towards a Real Character and a Philosophical Language
(London, 1668), Pt. I, ch. II, sect. I.

[1] [i.e. spoken by the people.]

CHANGE FOR THE BETTER

Since Learning began to flourish in our Nation, there have been more then ordinary Changes introduced in our Language: partly by new artificial Compositions; partly by enfranchising strange forein words, for their elegance and significancy, which now make one third part of our Language; and partly by refining and mollifying old words, for the more easie and graceful sound: by which means this last Century may be conjectured to have made a greater change in our Tongue, then any of the former, as to the addition of new words. *Ibid.* sect. II.

SPELLING

One special Circumstance which adds to the Curse of Babel is that difficulty which there is in all Languages, arising from the various Imperfections belonging to them, both in respect of 1. their first Elements or Alphabets, 2 their Words.

1. For *Alphabets*, they are all of them, in many respects, liable to just exception.

2. As to the Order of them, they are inartificial and confused, without any such methodical distribution as were requisite for their particular natures and differences; the Vowels and Consonants being promiscuously huddled together, without any distinction: Whereas in a regular Alphabet, the Vowels and Consonants should be reduced into Classes, according to their several kinds, with such an order of precedence and subsequence as their natures will bear . . . *Ibid.* ch. IV, sect. I.

[Alphabets are] Deficient . . . especially in regard of Vowels, of which there are 7 or 8 several kinds commonly used . . . though the Latin Alphabet take notice but of five, whereof two, namely (*i* and *u*) according to our English pronunciation of them, are not properly Vowels, but Diphthongs. And besides, that gradual difference amongst Vowels of long and short is not sufficiently provided for. The Ancients were wont to express a long Vowel by doubling the Character of it; as *Amaabam, Naata*. . . . For the ways used by us English for lengthning and abbreviating Vowels, viz. by adding *E* quiescent to the end of a word for prolonging a Syllable, and doubling the following Consonant for the shortning of a Vowel, as *Wane, Wann*; *Ware, Warr*, etc. or else by inserting some other Vowel, for the lengthning of it, as *Meat, Met*; *Read, Red*,

48

etc. both these are upon this account improper because the sign ought to be where the sound is. Nor would it be fit to express this by a distinct Character, because it denotes onely an accidental or gradual difference, as by an Accent; the chief use of Accents, for which they are necessary in ordinary speech, being to signifie Quantities and Elevations of voice.

Ibid. sect. II, 2

The letters C, S, T, are often used alike, to denote the same Power, and that both in English and French; and the letter (S) is most frequently used for (Z) which must needs be very improper. And, which is yet more irrational, some Letters of the same name and shape are used sometimes for Vowels, and sometimes for Consonants; as J, V, W, Y; which yet differ from one another *sicut corpus & anima*, and ought by no means to be confounded.

Ibid. sect. III, 2.

EQUIVOCAL WORDS

[Language is defective] In regard of Equivocals, which are of several significations, and therefore must needs render speech doubtful and obscure; and that argues a deficiency, or want of a sufficient number of words. These are either absolutely so, or in their figurative construction, or by reason of Phraseologies. . . .

So the word *Bill* signifies both a Weapon, a Bird's Beak, and a written Scroul: The word *Grave* signifies both Sober, and Sepulcher, and to Carve, etc.

As for the ambiguity of words by reason of Metaphor and Phraseology, this is in all instituted Languages so obvious and so various, that it is needless to give any instances of it; every Language having some peculiar phrases belonging to it, which, if they were to be translated verbatim into another Tongue, would seem wild and insignificant. In which our English doth too much abound, witness those words of *Break, Bring, Cast, Cleare, Come, Cut, Draw, Fall, Hand, Keep, Lay, make, Pass, Put, Run, Set, Stand, Take,* none of which have less than thirty or forty, and some of them about a hundred several senses, according to their use in Phrases, as may be seen in the Dictionary. And though the varieties of Phrases in Language may seem to contribute to the elegance and ornament of Speech; yet, like other affected ornaments, they prejudice the native simplicity of it, and contribute to the disguising of it with false appearances. Besides that, like other things of fashion, they are very changeable, every generation producing new ones; witness the Age, especially the late times, wherein this grand imposture of Phrases hath almost eaten out solid Knowledge in all professions; such men generally being of most esteem who are skilled in these Canting forms of speech, though in nothing else.   *Ibid.* sect. VI, I.

SPELLING REFORM

As to our own Language, several persons have taken much pains about the Orthography of it. That Learned Knight Sir Thomas Smith, Secretary to Queen Elizabeth, and sometime her Embassador into France, hath published an elegant Discourse in Latin, *De recta & emendata Linguae Anglicanae scriptione.* After him, this Subject was in another Discourse prosecuted by one of the Heralds, who calls himself Chester; who was followed by one Wade, that writ to the same purpose. After these, Bullaker endeavoured to add to, and alter divers things in those others that preceded him; who was succeeded in the same attempt by Alexander Gill, in his English Grammar. And yet so invincible is Custom, that still we retain the same errors and incongruities in writing which our Forefathers taught us.   *Ibid.* 4.

A UNIVERSAL LANGUAGE

That conceit which men have in their minds concerning a Horse or Tree, is the Notion or mental Image of that Beast, or natural thing, of such a nature, shape and use. The Names given to these in several Languages, are such arbitrary sounds or words, as Nations of men have agreed upon, either casually or designedly, to express their Mental notions of them. The Written word is the figure or picture of that Sound.

So that if men should generally consent upon the same way or manner of Expression, as they do agree in the same Notion, we should then be freed from that Curse in the Confusion of Tongues, with all the unhappy consequences of it.

Now this can onely be done, either by enjoyning some one Language and Character to be universally learnt and practised, (which is not to be expected, till some person attain to the Universal Monarchy; and perhaps would not be done then:) or else by proposing some such way as, by its facility and usefulness, (without the imposition of Authority)

might invite and ingage men to the learning of it; which is the thing
here attempted. *Ibid.* ch. v, sect. II.

DEFINITIONS OF GRAMMAR

1. Natural Grammar, (which may likewise be stiled Philosophical,
Rational, and Universal) should contain all such Grounds and Rules,
as do naturally and necessarily belong to the Philosophy of letters and
speech in the General.

2. Instituted and Particular Grammar, doth deliver the rules which
are proper and peculiar to any one Language in Particular; as about the
Inflexion of words, and the Government of cases, etc.

Op. cit. Pt. III, ch. I, sect. I.

TENSE AND MODE

The Tenses in instituted Languages are appropriated only to Verbs, yet
'tis very plain that according to the true Philosophy of speech, they
should likewise be ascribed to Substantives; And that this would in
many respects be a great advantage to Language. As there is *Amatio*, so
there should be *Amavitio* and *Amaturitio*, etc.

These kind of Auxiliary Particles, stiled Modes and Tenses, are in the
Modern Languages expressed by such servile words, as do not signifie
any compleat Act, but rather some respects and circumstances belonging to other Acts; and by that means have in them a natural fitness to be
subservient to the inflexion of other Integral words.

Ibid. ch. v, sect. III.

ACCIDENTAL DIFFERENCES OF WORDS

Concerning the Inflexion of them, which doth consist in the several
ways of varying the same word to sundry modes of signification. This
is not arbitrary, as it is used in several Languages; much less should the
rules to this purpose, which belong to the Latin, be applied to Vulgar
Tongues, to which they are not suited (as many Grammarians use to do)
but it ought to be founded upon the Philosophy of speech and such
Natural grounds, as do necessarily belong to Language.

Integral words are all capable of Inflexion.

I. Noun Substantives are inflected in a threefold respect.

1. By Number, Singular[1] and Plural which being more Intrinsecal to them, ought to be provided for in the Character or word it self, and not by an Affix.

2. By Gender, in things that are capable of Sex, which are naturally but two, Masculine and Feminine: These being less Intrinsical to the primary notion of the word, may be more properly expressed by affixes; and then the kind or species of every Animal (abstractedly from the respective Sexes of it) may be signifyed by the Radical word it self, without any sign of Sex, which will prevent much equivocalness.

3. By Cases, which is not so essential and natural to Substantives, as to be provided for in the word it self, by varying the Terminations of it; For though this course hath been used in the Greek and Latin: yet neither do the Oriental Tongues, Hebrew, Chaldee, Arabic, etc. nor those Occidental of French, Italian, Spanish; nor I think doth any Modern Tongue in the world this way express them.

The true notion of the Nominative case, is that which precedes the Verb, and the Accusative, that which follows the Verb; of which in speech that is suited to natural Structure and Syntax, there ought to be no other sign or note then the very order. As for the Genitive Case, the proper notion of that, is its following another Substantive *in regimine*: But because the following Substantive is not always governed by that which precedes; as *Urbs Roma, Rhenus Fluvius, Taxus arbor*, etc. therefore 'tis proper to have a Particle or Preposition for it, as our English (*Of*), and (*De*) in the *French, Italian, Spanish* . . . The Dative case is expressed by the Preposition (*To*) the *Vocative* by the Interjection of bespeaking (*O*) and the Ablative case by such a Preposition as denotes Formal or Instrumental cause, or manner of Doing. So that the true notion of the Genitive, Dative, Ablative Case, is nothing else but that obliquity in the sence of a Substantive, which is caused and signifyed by some Preposition annexed to it, as the Vocative is by an Interjection.

Ibid. ch. viii, sect. i, i.

IDIOM

That structure may be stiled *Customary* and figurative, which is used in the Phraseologies or forms of Speech, peculiar to several Languages, wherein words are put together according to a *Metaphorical* and tralatitious sense of them; as in those Latin Phrases, *Redigere in ordinem*, which

[1] [Text, *Singural*.]

signifies *Privare magistratu*; *E medio tollere* for *Occidere*. And so for those English Phrases of Breaking a jest, Hedging in a Debt, Taking ones heels and flying away. . . . All which ought to be rendered according to the natural sense and meaning intended by those Phrases; which is observed in the regular Translation of any Language. And he that would go about to render such forms of speech, according to the strict and natural sense of the words, could not reasonably expect to be understood in any other Language.

Ibid. ch. IX, sect. I, i.

WILLIAM HOLDER (1616–1698)

DIFFICULTIES OF REFORMING SPELLING

[We need a more phonetic spelling: but] In the mean time we are apt very unjustly to laugh at the uncouth Spelling in the writings of un-learned persons, who writing as they please, that is, using such Letters, as justly express the power or Sound of their Speech; yet, forsooth, we say write not *true English*, or *true French* etc. Whereas the Grammarians themselves, ought rather to be blamed, and derided for accommodating Words so ill with Letters, and Letters with so faulty Alphabets, that it requires almost as much pains to learn how to pronounce what is writ-ten, and to write what is spoken, as would serve to learn the Language it self, if Characters or Signs written were exactly accommodated to Speech. But, though it be true, that this so needless and unprofitable incumbrance of Learning might wholly be removed by rectified Alpha-bets, and setling a just correspondence between the Signs *Audible* and the Signs *Visible*, if such Alphabets and a regular usage of them could take place; yet it is not to be hoped or imagined, that the incongruous Alphabets, and Abuses of writing can ever be justled out of their Posses-sion of all Libraries and Books, and universal habit and practice of Man-kind. This were to imply, that all Books in being should be destroyed and abolished, being first new Printed after such rectified Alphabets; and that all the Age should be prevailed with, to take new pains to unlearn those habits, which have cost them so much labour.

Elements of Speech (1669), pp. 107–9.

CHRISTOPHER COOPER (d.˚1698)

ON GRAMMAR

It is the rule and foundation of speech, which is the channel of all arts and sciences, of Religion and Law, the picture of the spirit, the bond of society; by the use of reason and speech, men are distinguished from beasts without intelligence. It is enough for ordinary people to be instructed how to express their thoughts to be understood by others: but the learned ought to speak and write aptly and elegantly; and that is what grammar teaches, which makes clear the system and analogy of every vernacular, and having been spread through various nations, preserves it for ever from the injury of time. It purifies it of errors of speech and barbarism: it puts to flight difficulties which at first seem insuperable: for when the rules of Grammar are skilfully taught, any language can be more easily understood, more surely learnt, and longer kept in the memory.

Grammatica Linguæ Anglicanæ (1685).
(Translated from the Preface.)

STRANGE WORDS

Our language is so constituted that it is very easy to make new words or to adapt strange ones, so that there is no art or science which cannot be fully and copiously dealt with in English. But the greatest care ought to be taken, the advice of learned grammarians and the authority of the magistracy [government] should be sought before new or strange words should be admitted into *common* use: for this childish (shall I say mad?) affectation of words is absolutely blameworthy, when much more suitable ones could be drawn from our own fount; the affected words obscure the native propriety of the language, and make the language itself untrue to its own nature, confused, uncertain, and burdened with a useless weight of words.

Ibid. Preface, *De Copia*, sect. 1.

SYNONYMS

With so much abundance, we are given such a choice that there is nothing which cannot be fittingly expressed in our tongue; whereby not only can things be expressed in a neutral sense, but even the various attitudes towards them, and ideas about them, are firmly demonstrated.

Christopher Cooper (d. 1698)

For example, the nouns *Anguish, woe, sadness, heaviness, sorrow, trouble, dump, melancholy, agony,* indicate various degrees of soul-sickness. *Sad, heavy, sorrowful, cast down, bitter, doleful, ruful, pensive, dejected, disconsolat, tragical* are the adjectives. *Lamentable, deplorable* are passive and abstract. *Be-moan, be-wail, lament, moan, cry, complain* are verbs, *take in, take heavily,* are verbs of stronger meaning; *whimper, pule, whine,* of weaker: *vex, cut, cast down* imply activity. So *sin, fault, trespass, over-sight, failing, infirmity, dishonesty, transgression, crime, enormity, turpitude,* have some special difference as regards degree, purpose, method, consequence or something else: so synonyms serve not only for ornament but for use, especially in *precise speech,* in which much is comprehended in a few words, and many ideas are brought into play.   *Ibid. De Significantia.*

EXAMPLES OF 'BARBAROUS DIALECT', 1685

[a] If we wish to write accurately, we must avoid the barbarous dialect
[which says]

Bushop for *Bishop*	*shet* for *shut*
Chorles for *Charles*	*sarvice* for *service*
mought for *might*	*stomp* for *stamp*
meece for *mice*	*yerb* for *herba* [sic]
wuts for *oats*	

[b]

git for *get*	*shure* for *sure*
hundurd for *hundred*	*shugar* for *sugar*
sez for *saies*	*vitles* for *victuals*

[These are] spoken 'Facilitatis causa'.   *Ibid. cap. xix.*

VARIED SPELLINGS

[Cooper illustrates the varied spellings possible in his time:]

Apricock, abricot.	Licorice, liquorish.
Balet, balad.	Vat, fat.
Bankrupt, bankrout.	Yelk, yolk.
Clot, clod.	

Superfluous letters should be avoided.   *Ibid. cap. xx.*

GEORGE HICKES (1642–1715)

ON THE NOUN IN ANGLO-SAXON

The Noun is either a Noun Substantive or a Noun Adjective. The Substantive is either simple or compound: Simple, such as *wite*, punishment, *hus*, house, *hiwe*, house or household, *gedale*, division. Compound: such as *wite-hus*, house of punishments, *hiw-gedale*, divorce, *henne-aeg*, hen's egg (from *henne* & *aeg*) *butan an henne-aeg*, nisi unum gallinae ovum (Bed. H.E. p. 226). And as no language delights more in compounds, so none (not even Greek) is more felicitous in them than Anglo-Saxon; so that it is in the habit of expressing every kind of condition and consideration without obscurity by its unions of terms clearly and elegantly. Even those who have only a beginner's knowledge of Anglo-Saxon will notice the expressive elegance of these compounds, not without great delight. Here are a few examples: names used by Caedmon of the Ark of Noah, playing with their variety. *Mere-hus*, sea-house, *wudu-faesten*, *wooden fortress. Mere-cieste*, sea-ark, *sund-reced*, sea-hall, *waeg-bord*, *tent on the waves, waeg-þele*, tent on the waves, *stream-weall, wall of the waves, hrof-gefor*,[1] *moving-roof.* To which add *lif-frea, lord of life, gast-gedal, separation of spirit* i.e. *death. eþel-stol, homeland. heolster-sceado, cave of shadows,* i.e. *chaos.* It is to be observed that the first word in noun compounds . . . has the nature of an Adjective, and should be rendered by an Adjective in Latin: or failing an Adjective, by a Genitive or periphrasis equivalent to the Adjective e.g. *Irenn-bend, vinculum ferreum.*

Nouns in Anglo-Saxon vary in their cases, as in Greek and Latin. Substantives vary (so far as I have been able to observe hitherto) in six ways, so there may be said to be six declensions in Anglo-Saxon.

[The six type-words are *smið, witega, andȝit, word, wiln, sunu*. Nouns of relationship and *fot, man, æg* and *cealf* are noted as irregular, and their plurals recorded.]

The 1st Declension consists of nouns that make the genitive singular in *es*, dative in *e*, nominative plural in *as*, genitive in *a*, and dative in *um*: as,

	sing.	plur.
nom.	smið	*smiðas
gen.*	smiðes	smiða

---

[1] [This seems to be a mis-reading: cf. *Genesis* 1360 *under hrof gefor*, where *gefor* is a verb.]

dat.	smiðe	smiðum
acc.	smið	smiðas
voc.	eala þu smið	eala ʒe smiðas
abl.	smiðe	smiðum

** Hence in our language the genitive singular and nominative plural of substantives end in *s* or *es*: as in *stones* which means *lapidis* and *lapides*.

Institutiones Grammaticae Anglo-Saxonicae et Maeso-Gothicae (1689)
(Text in Latin: the Anglo-Saxon words printed
in Anglo-Saxon characters), ch. III.

JOHN DRYDEN (1631–1700)

LATIN LOANS

I will not excuse but justifie my self for one pretended Crime, with
which I am liable to be charg'd by false Criticks, not only in this Translation, but in many of my Original Poems; that I latinize too much.
'T is true, that when I find an English word, significant and sounding, I
neither borrow from the Latin, or any other Language: But when I want
at home, I must seek abroad.

If sounding Words are not of our growth and Manufacture, who shall
hinder me to Import them from a Foreign Country? I carry not out the
Treasure of the Nation, which is never to return: but what I bring from
Italy, I spend in England: Here it remains, and here it circulates; for if
the Coyn be good, it will pass from one hand to another. I Trade both
with the Living and the Dead, for the enrichment of our Native Language. We have enough in England to supply our necessity; but if we
will have things of Magnificence and Splendour, we must get them by
Commerce. Poetry requires Ornament, and that is not to be had from
our Old Teuton Monosyllables; therefore if I find any Elegant Word
in a Classick Author, I propose it to be naturaliz'd, by using it my self:
and if the Publick approves of it, the Bill passes. But every Man cannot
distinguish betwixt Pedantry and Poetry: Every Man therefore is not
fit to innovate. Upon the whole matter, a Poet must first be certain that
the Word he wou'd Introduce is Beautiful in the Latin; and is to consider, in the next place, whether it will agree with the English idiom:
After this, he ought to take the Opinion of judicious Friends, such as
are Learned in both Languages: And lastly, since no Man is infallible,
let him use this License very sparingly; for if too many Foreign Words

are pour'd in upon us, it looks as if they were design'd not to assist the Natives, but to Conquer them.

The Works of Virgil translated into English Verse by Mr Dryden.
(1697). Dedication of the *Æneid*.[1]

LINGUISTIC COMPACTNESS

He [Virgil] studies brevity more than any other poet; but he had the advantage of a language wherein much may be comprehended in a little space. We, and all the modern tongues, have more articles and pronouns, besides signs of tenses and cases, and other barbarities on which our speech is built by the fault of our forefathers. . . .

This inconvenience is common to all modern tongues, and this alone constrains us to employ more words than the ancients needed.

Op. cit. (edition of 1792), pp. 200–1.

MONOSYLLABLES

[Dryden complains of] monosyllables . . . , and those clogged with consonants, which are the dead weight of our mother-tongue. It is possible, I confess, though it rarely happens, that a verse of monosyllables may sound harmoniously. . . .

. . . it seldom happens but a monosyllable line turns verse to prose, and even that prose is rugged and unharmonious. *Ibid.* p. 199.

DANIEL DEFOE (1660?–1731)

A PROJECTED ENGLISH ACADEMY

The peculiar Study of the Academy of Paris, has been to Refine and Correct their own Language; which they have done to that happy degree, that we see it now spoken in all the Courts of Christendom, as the Language allow'd to be most universal.

I had the Honour once to be a Member of a small Society, who seem'd to offer at this Noble Design in England. But the Greatness of the Work, and the Modesty of the Gentlemen concern'd, prevail'd with them to desist an Enterprize which appear'd too great for Private Hands to under-

[1] [The same passage, with different spelling and capitalization, may perhaps more easily be referred to in the edition of 1792, vol. II, p. 212. The pages of the first edition are unnumbered.]

take. We want indeed a Richlieu to commence such a Work: . . . The English Tongue is a Subject not at all less worthy the Labour of such a Society than the French, and capable of a much greater Perfection. The Learned among the French will own, That the Comprehensiveness of Expression is a Glory in which the English Tongue not only Equals but Excels its Neighbours. . . .

[Defoe proposes] That a Society be erected by the King himself, if his Majesty thought fit, and composed of none but Persons of the first Figure in Learning; and 'twere to be wish'd our Gentry were so much Lovers of Learning, that Birth might always be join'd with Capacity.

The Work of this Society shou'd be to encourage Polite Learning, to polish and refine the English Tongue, and advance the so much neglected Faculty of Correct Language, to establish Purity and Propriety of Stile, and to purge it from all the Irregular Additions that Ignorance and Affectation have introduc'd; and all those Innovations in Speech, if I may call them such, which some Dogmatic Writers have the Confidence to foster upon their Native Language, as if their Authority were sufficient to make their own Fancy legitimate.

By such a Society I dare say the true Glory of our English Stile wou'd appear; and among all the Learned Part of the World, be esteem'd, as it really is, the Noblest and most Comprehensive of all the Vulgar Languages in the World.

Into this Society should be admitted none but Persons Eminent for Learning, and yet none, or but very few, whose Business or Trade was Learning: For I may be allow'd, I suppose, to say, We have seen many great Scholars, meer Learned Men, and Graduates in the last Degree of Study, whose English has been far from Polite, full of Stiffness and Affectation, hard Words, and long unusual Coupling of Syllables and Sentences, which sound harsh and untuneable to the Ear, and shock the Reader both in Expression and Understanding.

In short, There should be room in this Society for neither Clergyman, Physician, or Lawyer. Not that I wou'd put an Affront upon the Learning of any of those Honourable Employments, much less upon their Persons: But if I do think that their several Professions do naturally and severally prescribe Habits of Speech to them peculiar to their Practice, and prejudicial to the Study I speak of, I believe I do them no wrong. Nor do I deny but there may be, and now are among some of all those Professions, Men of Stile and Language, great Masters of English, whom few men will undertake to Correct; and where such do at any time appear, their extraordinary Merit shou'd find them a Place in this Society; but it shou'd be rare, and upon very extraordinary Occasions, that such be admitted.

I wou'd therefore have this Society wholly compos'd of Gentlemen; whereof Twelve to be of the Nobility, if possible, and Twelve Private Gentlemen, and a Class of Twelve to be left open for meer Merit, let it be found in who or what sort it would, which should lye as the Crown of their Study, who have done something eminent to deserve it. The Voice of this Society should be sufficient Authority for the Usage of Words, and sufficient also to expose the Innovations of other mens Fancies; they shou'd preside with a sort of Judicature over the Learning of the Age, and have liberty to Correct and Censure the Exorbitance of Writers, especially of Translators. The Reputation of this Society wou'd be enough to make them the allow'd Judges of Stile and Language; and no Author wou'd have the Impudence to Coin without their Authority. Custom, which is now our best Authority for Words, wou'd always have its Original here, and not be allow'd without it. There shou'd be no more occasion to search for Derivations and Constructions, and 'twou'd be as Criminal then to Coin Words, as Money.

The Exercises of this Society wou'd be Lectures on the English Tongue, Essays on the Nature, Original, Usage, Authorities and Differences of Words, on the Propriety, Purity, and Cadence of Stile, and of the Politeness and Manner in writing; Reflections upon Irregular Usages, and Corrections of Erroneous Customs in Words; and in short, every thing that wou'd appear necessary to the bringing our English Tongue to a due Perfection, and our Gentlemen to a Capacity of Writing like themselves; to banish Pride and Pedantry, and silence the Impudence and Impertinence of Young Authors, whose Ambition is to be known, tho' it be by their Folly.   *An Essay upon Several Projects.*
'Of Academies' (1702), pp. 228 ff.

ON SWEARING

I ask leave here for a Thought or two about that Inundation Custom has made upon our Language and Discourse by Familiar Swearing, and I place it here, because Custom has so far prevail'd in this foolish Vice, that a man's Discourse is hardly agreeable without it; and some have taken upon them to say, It is a pity it shou'd not be lawful, 'tis such a Grace in a man's speech, and adds so much Vigour to his Language. . . .

Daniel Defoe (1660?-1731)

I am not about to argue any thing of their[1] being sinful and unlawful, as forbid by Divine Rules; let the Parson alone to tell you that, who has, no question, said as much to as little purpose in this Case as in any other: But I am of the opinion, that there is nothing so Impertinent, so Insignificant, so Sensless and Foolish, as our Vulgar way of Discourse, when mix'd with Oaths and Curses; and I wou'd only recommend a little Consideration to our Gentlemen, who have Sense and Wit enough, and wou'd be asham'd to speak Nonsense in other things, but value themselves upon their Parts; I wou'd but ask them to put into Writing the Common-Places of their Discourse, and read them over again, and examine the English, the Cadence, the Grammar of them; then let them turn them into Latin, or translate them into any other Language, and but see what a Jargon and Confusion of Speech they make together.

Ibid. p. 238.

LOCAL DIALECT

It cannot pass my Observation here, that, when we are come this Length from London, the Dialect of the English Tongue, or the Country-way of expressing themselves, is not easily understood. It is the same in many Parts of England besides, but in none in so gross a Degree as in this Part. As this Way of boorish Speech is in Ireland called, *The Brougue upon the Tongue*, so here it is named *Jouring*. It is not possible to explain this fully by Writing, because the Difference is not so much in the Orthography, as in the Tone and Accent; their abridging the Speech, *Cham*, for *I am*; *Chil*, for *I will*; *Don*, for *do on*, or *put on*; and *Doff*, for *do off*, or *put off*; and the like.

I cannot omit a short Story here on this Subject: Coming to a Relation's House, who was a Schoolmaster at Martock in Somersetshire, I went into his School to beg the Boys, or rather the Master, a Play-day, as is usual in such Cases. I observed one of the lowest Scholars was reading his Lesson to the Usher in a Chapter in the Bible. I sat down by the Master, till the Boy had read it out, and observed the Boy read a little oddly in the Tone of the Country, which made me the more attentive; because, on Inquiry, I found that the Words were the same, and the Orthography the same, as in all our Bibles. I observed also the Boy read it out with his Eyes still on the Book, and his Head, like a mere Boy, moving from Side to Side, as the Lines reached cross the Columns of the

[1] [i.e. oaths, etc.]

Book: His Lesson was in the *Canticles of Solomon*; the Words these; 'I have put off my Coat; how shall I put it on? I have washed my Feet; how shall I defile them?' The Boy read thus, with his Eyes, as I say, full on the Text: 'Chav a doffed my Coot; how shall I don't? Chav a washed my Feet; how shall I moil 'em?'

How the dexterous Dunce could form his Mouth to express so readily the Words (which stood right printed in the Book) in his Country Jargon, I could not but admire.[1]

We likewise see their Jouring speech even upon their Monuments and Grave-stones; as for Example, in some of the Church-yards of the City of Bristol, I saw this Poetry after some other Lines—

> And when that thou dost hear of Thick,[2]
> Think of the Glass that runneth quick.

> *A Tour thro' Somerset. A Tour through the Whole Island*
> *of Great Britain* (from the edition of 1769, vol. I,
> pp. 356–7. First published 1724–7).

THOMAS DYCHE (fl. 1719)

COMMENTS FROM
AN EIGHTEENTH-CENTURY SPELLING BOOK

[*C* is stated to be silent in *verdict, perfect, perfected, perfectness*, but sounded in *perfection, perfective*; *ch* is soft in *stomachic*; *d* is silent in *ribband*.]

If Nouns in *E* Final take *s* after them, with an Apostrophy before it, it stands for *his* and notes Possession. . . . If without an Apostrophy, it makes the Plural Number.

If Verbs, that end in *E* Final take *s* after them, it is abbreviated from -eth.

[*G* is sounded in *condign*
Hough = hoff
No *H* sound in *herb, Humphrey*]

I is sounded like *ee* in *oblidge, Magazine, Machine*. . . .

N.B. The tail'd J, by some Authors is called j consonant, and by others Jod, to distinguish from the vowel I, which is really quite another Letter, and differs both in Sound and Shape.

But because the Hebrew Names of Letters are not all received into

---

[1] [=be astonished at.]   [2] [That.]

our Alphabet, I take the Liberty to call it *ja*, as most agreeing with the other Names of our English Letters.

L is not sounded in *almost, Lincoln, Bristol, Holborn*
M is sounded like *n* in the word *Accompt* (Account)
N is not heard in *Kiln*
O is transplaced in *iron* (iorn) *saffron* (safforn)
O is lost in these words, *Coroner* (Crowner) *damosel* (damsel) *feoffè* (feffè), *Nicolas* (Niclas) *carrion* (carrin) *chariot* (charit)
The *a* is lost in *Calais* (Callis)
[*Veil, either, key, convey* have the same sound]
oi and *oy* have a peculiar Sound, expressible by no other Letters, from which they seldom or never vary. . . .
In some Words *ou* has the sound of *oo*; as, *soup* (soop) *stroud* (strood) *Cowper* (Cooper)
Oa is sounded like au, in *broad, abroad, groat*.

Let Proper Names of Persons, Places, Ships, Rivers, etc, be always distinguished by beginning with a Capital or great Letter. 'Tis esteemed Ornamental to begin any Substantive in the Sentence with a Capital, if it bear some considerable Stress of the Authors Sense upon it, to make it the more Remarkable and Conspicuous. 'Tis grown Customary in Printing to begin every Substantive with a Capital; but in my Opinion, it is unnecessary, and hinders that remarkable Distinction intended by a Capital. . . .

If any notable Saying or Passage of an Author, be quoted in his own Words, it begins with a Capital, tho' it be not immediately after a full stop. . . .

K, seems to be unnecessary in the End of Words not purely English; as, Music, Arithmetic, Logic, Catholic, Fabric, rather than Musick. . . . The long ſ[1] must never be used at the End of a Word, nor immediately after a short s. X should be used instead of ct where it appears to have been in the Original; as, Reflexion, Connexion, rather than Reflection, Connection.

A Guide to the English Tongue, in Two Parts (second edition, 1710)
(quoted from the fourteenth edition, 1729).

[1] [This distribution of long and short *s* has not been kept in this collection.]

ADVANTAGES AND DISADVANTAGES
OF OUR HISTORICAL SPELLING

I have been at the Pains . . . to compare foreign Words with their Originals, in order to fix the right Spelling of them; and in that Search I have discover'd, that our Language, over and besides what it owes to the Ancients, is much indebted to the Italian, but more abundantly to the French, which I attribute to the Norman Conquest. However, it's plain, tho' this Borrowing from foreign Language is, for the most part, both an Ornament and Enrichment to our own; yet it renders our Spelling the more difficult, inasmuch as many of those Words are now politely sounded after the foreign way, which is very different from that harsh and uncertain Method, whereby the English is pronounced.

A Dictionary[1] *of all the Words Commonly Us'd*
in the English Tongue (1723). Preface.

COMMON SENSE AND CONVENTION

By the leave of my good Friends, the Printers, and Correctors of the Press, I would propose, not to use many Letters in a Word, when fewer may do as well. Hence (ck) need not be together in the end of such borrow'd Words, as, *concentric*, *Lyric*, *magnetic*: but I retain it in all English Words for Antiquity's sake. One (l) may commonly serve at the End of a Word, as well as two; so I hope the Liberty I have taken that way may be pardonable. I think also, that (e) final may be left out, when it does not lengthen a syllable; as in *doctrine*, *rapine*, *humane*,[2] *handsome*, etc. There are some Words sounded so differently from their Letters, that I think the best way would be to spell them by the Ear. For Instance, I approve these Words, *Count*, *account*, *accountant*, *gage*, *gager*, *Lievtenant*, *skeptic*, *skeleton*, rather than *Compt*, *accompt*, *accomptant*, *gauge*, *gauger*, *Lieutenant*, *sceptic*, *sceleton*. . . .

Latin Substantives in (-*or*) become English ones in (-*our*); tho' I think that (u) to be unnecessary, because, when the Word increases, it drops; as *humour*, *humorist*, *humorsom*: But to propose my single Opinion against the public Vogue, I must confess, is a hazardous Enterprize; for Custom will bear a Man down, unless he find a good Number of Candid Friends to support him.

Ibid.

[1] [Really a spelling-list.]
[2] [Our distinction between *human* and *humane* dates from after 1700.]

JAMES GREENWOOD (d. 1737) AND SIR RICHARD STEELE (1672–1729)

GRAMMAR

... I was startled ... and grieved to see our Sterling English Language fallen into the Hands of Clippers and Coyners. That mutilated Epistle,[1] consisting of *Hippo*, *Rep's*, and such-like enormous Curtailings, was a mortifying Spectacle. ...

I take our corrupt Ways of Writing to proceed from the Mistakes and wrong Measures in our common Methods of Education, which I always looked upon as one of our National Grievances, and a Singularity that renders us no less than our Situation,—Penitus toto divisos Orbe Britannos. ...

[Grammatical error] is a necessary Consequence of our Mismanagement in that Province.

For can any Thing be more absurd than our Way of Proceeding in this Part of Literature? To push tender Wits into the intricate Mazes of Grammar, and a *Latin* Grammar? To learn an unknown Art by an unknown Tongue? To carry them a dark Round-about Way to let them in at a Back-Door? Whereas by teaching them first the Grammar of their Mother-Tongue (so easy to be learned) their Advance to the Grammars of Latin and Greek would be gradual and easy; but our precipitate Way of hurrying them over such a Gulph before we have built them a Bridge to it, is a Shock to their weak Understandings, which they seldom, or very late, recover. ...

The Liberal Arts and Sciences are all beautiful as the *Graces*; nor has Grammar (the severe Mother of all) so frightful a Face of her Own; 'tis the Vizzard put upon it that scares Children. She is made to speak hard Words that to them sound like Conjuring. Let her talk intelligibly, and they will listen to her. ...

It has been the Practice of wisest Nations to learn their own Language by stated Rules, to avoid the Confusion that would follow from leaving it to vulgar Use. Our English Tongue (says a learned Man)[2] is the most determinate in its Construction, and reducible to the fewest Rules: Whatever Language has less Grammar in it, is not intelligible, and whatever has more, all that it has more is superfluous; for which Reasons

---

[1] [In *The Tatler*, no. 230, 27 September 1710, by Swift.]
[2] [M. Lewis, in the Preface to *Grammatica Puerilis* (1674).]

he would have it made the Foundation of learning *Latin*, and all other Languages.

To speak and write without Absurdity the Language of ones Country, is commendable in Persons of all Stations, and to some indispensibly necessary; and to this Purpose, I would recommend above all Things the having a Grammar of our Mother-Tongue first taught in our Schools, which would facilitate our Youths learning their Latin and Greek Grammars. . . .   *The Tatler*, no. 234, 6 October 1710.

JOSEPH ADDISON (1672–1719)

ENGLISH AN ENEMY TO LOQUACITY

The English delight in Silence more than any other European Nation, if the Remarks which are made on us by Foreigners are true. Our Discourse is not kept up in Conversation, but falls into more Pauses and Intervals than in our Neighbouring Countries; as it is observed, that the matter of our writings is thrown much closer together, and lies in a narrower Compass than is usual in the Works of Foreign Authors: For, to favour our Natural Taciturnity, when we are obliged to utter our Thoughts, we do it in the shortest way we are able, and give as quick a Birth to our Conceptions as possible.

This Humour shews itself in several Remarks that we may make upon the English Language. As first of all by its abounding in Monosyllables, which gives us an Opportunity of delivering our Thoughts in few Sounds. This indeed takes off from the Elegance of our Tongue, but at the same time expresses our Ideas in the readiest manner, and consequently answers the first Design of Speech better than the Multitude of Syllables, which make the Words of other Languages more Tunable and Sonorous. . . .

In the next place we may observe, that where the words are not Monosyllables, we often make them so, as much as lies in our Power, by our Rapidity of Pronunciation; as it generally happens in most of our long words which are derived from the Latin, where we contract the length of the Syllables that gives them a grave and solemn Air in their own Language, to make them more proper for Dispatch, and more conformable to the Genius of our Tongue. This we may find in a Multitude of Words, as *Liberty, Conspiracy, Theatre, Orator*, etc.

Joseph Addison (1672-1719)

The same natural Aversion to Loquacity has of late Years made a very considerable Alteration in our Language, by closing in one Syllable the Termination of our Præterperfect Tense, as in these Words *drown'd*, *walk'd*, *arriv'd* for *drowned*, *walked*, *arrived*, which has very much disfigured the Tongue, and turned a tenth part of our smoothest Words into so many Clusters of Consonants. This is the more remarkable, because the want of Vowels in our Language has been the general Complaint of our politest Authors, who nevertheless are the Men that have made these Retrenchments, and consequently very much increased our former Scarcity. . . .

I think we may add to the fore-going Observation, the Change which has happened in our Language, by the Abbreviation of several Words that are terminated in *eth*, by substituting an *s* in the room of the last Syllable, as in *drowns*, *walks*, *arrives*, and innumerable other Words, which in the Pronunciation of our Fore-fathers were *drowneth*, *walketh*, *arriveth*. This has wonderfully multiplied a Letter which was before too frequent in the English Tongue, and added to that hissing in our Language, which is taken so much Notice of by Foreigners; but at the same time humours our Taciturnity, and eases us of many superfluous Syllables.

I might here observe, that the same single Letter on many Occasions does the Office of a whole Word, and represents the *His* and *Her* of our Fore-fathers. . . .[1]

[We retain] the old Termination in Writing and in all the solemn Offices of our Religion.

As in the Instances I have given we have epitomized many of our particular Words to the Detriment of our Tongue, so on other Occasions we have drawn two Words into one, which has likewise very much untuned our Language, and clogged it with Consonants, as *mayn't*, *can't*, *shan't*, *won't*, and the like, for *may not*, *can not*, *shall not*, *will not*, etc.

It is perhaps this Humour of speaking no more than we needs must, which has so miserably curtailed some of our Words, that in familiar Writings and Conversations they often lose all but their first Syllables, as in *mob.*, *rep.*, *pos.*, *incog.* and the like; and as all ridiculous Words make their first Entry into a Language by familiar Phrases, I dare not answer for these that they will not in time be looked upon as a part of our Tongue.

[1] [Cf. Charles Butler, *English Grammar* (1634), vol. III, ii, who points out that 'my master's son is a child' is not derived from 'my master his son', which would be just as good as if in Latin we said '*Heri ejus filius*' for *Heri filius*.]

We see some of our Poets have been so indiscreet as to imitate *Hudibras's* Doggrel Expressions in their serious Compositions, by throwing out the signs of our Substantives, which are essential to the English Language. Nay, this Humour of shortning our Language had once run so far, that some of our celebrated Authors, among whom we may reckon Sir Roger L'Estrange in particular, began to prune their Words of all superfluous Letters, as they termed them, in order to adjust the Spelling to the Pronunciation; which would have confounded all our Etymologies, and have quite destroyed our Tongue. . . .

There is another Particular in our Language which is a great Instance of our Frugality of Words, and that is the suppressing of several Particles which must be produced in other Tongues to make a Sentence intelligible: This often perplexes the best writers, when they find the Relatives *whom, which* or *they*, at their Mercy, whether they may have Admission or not; and will never be decided till we have something like an Academy, that by the best Authorities and Rules drawn from the Analogy of Languages shall settle all Controversies between Grammar and Idiom. . . .

The Spectator (4 August 1711)
(from the edition of 1739).

MODES OF ADDRESS

An empty Man of a great Family is a Creature that is scarce conversible. You read his Ancestry in his Smile, in his Air, in his Eye-brow. He has indeed nothing but his Nobility to give Employment to his Thoughts. Rank and Precedency are the important Points which he is always discussing within himself. A Gentleman of this Turn begun a Speech in one of King Charles's Parliaments: 'Sir, I had the Honour to be born at a time'[1]—upon which a rough honest Gentleman took him up short, 'I would fain know what that Gentleman means, Is there any one in this House that has not had the Honour to be born as well as himself?' The good Sense which reigns in our Nation has pretty well destroyed this starched Behaviour among Men who have seen the World, and know that every Gentleman will be treated upon a Foot of Equality. But there are many who have had their Education among Women, Dependants or Flatterers, that lose all the Respect, which would otherwise be paid them, by being too assiduous in procuring it.

My Lord Froth has been so Educated in Punctilio, that he governs

[1] [Inverted commas replace the italics of the original.]

himself by a Ceremonial in all the ordinary Occurrences of Life. He Measures out his Bow to the Degree of the Person he converses with. I have seen him in every Inclination of the Body, from a familiar Nod to the low Stoop in the Salutation Sign. I remember five of us, who were acquainted with one another, met together one Morning at his Lodgings, when a Wag of the Company was saying, it would be worth while to observe how he would distinguish us at his first Entrance. Accordingly he no sooner came into the Room, but casting his Eye about, 'My Lord such a one,' says he, 'your most humble Servant. Sir Richard, your humble servant. Your Servant Mr. Ironside. Mr Ducker, how do you do? Hah! Frank, are you there?'

The Guardian (18 August 1713).

SIR RICHARD STEELE (1672–1729)

SPELLING[1]

I came Yesterday into the Parlour, where I found Mrs. Cornelia, my Lady's third Daughter, all alone, reading a Paper, which, as I afterwards found, contained a Copy of Verses, upon Love and Friendship. . . . By the Hand, at first sight, I could not guess whether they came from a Beau or a Lady, but having put on my spectacles, and perused them carefully, I found by some peculiar Modes in Spelling, and a certain Negligence in Grammar, that it was a Female Sonnet.

Ibid. (28 March 1713).

MISAPPLICATION OF TERMS

As the World now goes, we have no adequate Idea of what is meant by *Gentlemanly*, *Gentleman-like*, or *much of a Gentleman*; you can't be cheated at Play, but it is certainly done by *a very Gentleman-like Man*; you can't be deceived in your Affairs, but it was done in some *Gentlemanly Manner*. . . . Here is a very pleasant Fellow, a Correspondent of mine, that puts in for that Appellation even to High-way Men. . . .

Ibid. (24 April 1713).

[1] [This passage is ascribed to Steele in the edition by J. Nichols (1797) but the ascription is questioned by Nathan Drake in his *Essays Illustrative of the Tatler, The Spectator, and The Guardian* (1814).]

ALEXANDER POPE (1688–1744)

ARCHAISM

As Simplicity is the distinguishing Characteristick of Pastoral, Virgil hath been thought guilty of too Courtly a Style; his·Language is perfectly pure, and he often forgets he is among Peasants. I have frequently wondered that since he was so conversant in the Writings of Ennius, he had not imitated the Rusticity of the Doric, as well, by the help of the old obsolete Roman Language, as Philips hath by the antiquated English: For Example, might he not have said *Quoi* instead of *Cui*; *Quoijum* for *Cujum*; *volt* for *vult*, etc. as well as our Modern hath *Welladay* for *Alas*, *Whilome* for *of Old*, *make mock* for *deride*, and *witless Younglings* for *simple Lambs* etc. by which Means he had attained as much of the Air of Theocritus as Philips hath of Spencer. *Ibid.* (27 April 1713).

HOW TO MAKE AN EPIC POEM

For the Language. (I mean the Diction.) Here it will do Well to be an Imitator of Milton, for you'll find it easier to imitate him in this than any thing else. Hebraisms and Grecisms are to be found in him, without the Trouble of Learning the Languages. I knew a Painter, who (like our Poets) had no Genius, making his Dawbings be thought Originals by setting them in the Smoak: You may in the same manner give the venerable Air of Antiquity to your Piece, by darkening it up and down with Old English. With this you may be easily furnished upon any Occasion, by the Dictionary commonly Printed at the end of Chaucer.

Ibid. (10 June 1713).

? LAURENCE EUSDEN (1688–1730)

ON TRANSLATION

An eminent Prelate of our Church observes that there is no way of Writing so proper, for the refining and polishing a Language as the translating of Books into it, if he who undertakes it has a competent Skill of the one Tongue, and is a Master of the other. When a Man writes his own Thoughts, the Heat of his Fancy, and the Quickness of his Mind, carry him so much after the Notions themselves, that for the most part he is too warm to judge of the Aptness of Words, and the Justness of Figures; so that he either neglects these too much or overdoes them: But when a Man translates, he has none of these Heats about him; and therefore the French took no ill Method, when they intended to reform and beautifie their Language, in setting their best Writers on Work to translate the Greek and Latin authors into it. Thus far this Learned Prelate. And another lately deceas'd, tells us, that the way of leaving verbal Translations, and chiefly regarding the Sense and Genius of the Author, was scarce heard of in England before this present Age. As for the difficulty of translating well, every one, I believe, must allow my Lord Roscommon to be in the right, when he says,

> 'Tis true, Composing is the nobler Part,
> But good Translation is no easie Art;
> For tho' Materials have long since been found,
> Yet both your Fancy, and your Hands are bound;
> And by improving what was writ before,
> Invention labours less, but Judgment more.

Dryden judiciously Remarks, that a Translator is to make his Author appear as charming as possibly he can, provided he maintains his Character, and makes him not unlike himself. And a too close and servile Imitation, which the same Poet calls treading on the Heels of an Author, is deservedly laughed at by Sir John Denham. I conceive it, says he, a vulgar Error in translating Poets, to affect being *fidus interpres*: Let that Care be with them who deal in Matters of Fact, or Matters of Faith; but whosoever aims at it in Poetry, as he attempts what is not required, so shall he never perform what he attempts; for 'tis not his Business alone to translate Language into Language, but Poesie into Poesie; and Poesie is of so subtle a Spirit, that in pouring out of one Language into another, it will all evaporate, and if a new Spirit is not added in the Transfusion, there will remain nothing but a caput mortuum, there being certain Graces and Happinesses peculiar to every Language, which give Life and Energy to the Words: And whosoever offers at verbal Translations, shall have the Misfortune of the young Traveller, who lost his own Language abroad, and brought home no other instead of it. For the Grace of the Latin will be lost by being turned into English words, and the Grace of the English by being turned into the Latin Phrase.   *Ibid.* (18 September 1713).

English Examined

ANTHONY ASHLEY COOPER, 3rd EARL OF SHAFTESBURY (1671–1713)

DISCORD IN LANGUAGE

But so much are our British Poets taken up, in seeking out that monstrous Ornament which we call Rhyme, that 'tis no wonder if other Ornaments, and real Graces are unthought of, and left unattempted. . . . 'Tis a shame to our Authors, that in their elegant Stile and metred Prose, there shou'd not be found a peculiar Grace and Harmony, resulting from a more natural and easy Disengagement of their Periods, and from a careful avoiding the Encounter of the shocking Consonants and jarring Sounds to which our Language is so unfortunately subject. § They have of late, it's true, reform'd in some measure the gouty Joints and Darning-work of *Whereunto*'s, *Whereby*'s, *Thereof*'s, *Therewith*'s, and the rest of this kind; by which, complicated Periods are so curiously strung or hook'd on, one to another, after the long-spun manner of the Bar, or Pulpit. But to take into consideration no real Accent, or Cadency of Words, no Sound or Measure of Syllables; to put together, at one time, a Set of Compounds of the longest Greek or Latin Termination; and at another, to let whole Verses, and those too of our heroick and longest sort, pass currently in Monosyllables: is, methinks, no slender Negligence. If single Verses at the head, or in the most emphatical places, of the most considerable Works, can admit of such a Structure, and pass for truly harmonious and poetical in this negligent form; I see no reason why more Verses than one or two, of the same formation, shou'd not be as well admitted; or why an un-interrupted Succession of these well-strung Monosyllables might not be allow'd to clatter after one another, like the Hammers of a Paper-Mill, without any breach of Musick, or prejudice to the Harmony of our Language. But if Persons who have gone no farther than a Smith's Anvil to gain an Ear, are yet likely, on fair trial, to find a plain defect in these Ten-Monosyllable Heroicks; it wou'd follow, methinks, that even a Prose-Author, who attempts to write politely, shou'd endeavour to confine himself within those Bounds, which can never, without breach of Harmony, be exceeded in any just Metre, or agreeable Pronunciation.

Characteristics (1714), Miscellany v, ch. i, pp. 263–6.

ELIZABETH ELSTOB (1683–1756)

IN DEFENCE OF ANGLO-SAXON

This hath often occasion'd my Admiration, that those Persons, who talk so much, of the Honour of our Countrey, of the correcting, improving and ascertaining of our Language, shou'd dress it up in a Character so very strange and ridiculous; or to think of improving it to any degree of Honour and Advantage, by divesting it of the Ornaments of Antiquity, or separating it from the Saxon Root, whose Branches were so copious and numerous. But it is very remarkable how Ignorance will make Men bold, and presume to declare that unnecessary, which they will not be at the pains to render useful. . . .

"The Saxons [say the critics] if we may credit Dr. Hickes, had various Terminations to their Words, at least two in every Substantive singular; whereas we have no Word now in use, except the personal Names that has so. Thus Dr. Hickes has made six several Declensions of the Saxon Names: He gives them three Numbers; a Singular, Dual and Plural: We have no Dual Number, except perhaps in Both["]: . . . I would ask these Gentlemen, and why not credit Dr. Hickes? Is he not as much to be believ'd as those Gentlemen, who have transcribed so plain an Evidence of the six Declensions to shew the positive Unreasonableness and unwarrantable Contradiction of their Disbelief? Did he make those six Declensions? or rather, did he not find them in the Language, and take so much pains to teach others to distinguish them, who have Modesty enough to be taught? They are pleased to say we have no Word now in use that admits of Cases or Terminations. But let us ask them, what they think of these Words, *God's Word, Man's Wisdom*, the *Smith's Forge*, and innumerable Instances more. For in *God's Word*, etc. is not the Termination *s* a plain Indication of a Genitive case, wherein the Saxon *e* is omitted? For example, *Godes Word, Mannes Wisdom, Smiðes Heorð.* Some will say, that were better supplied by *his* or *hers* as *Man his Thought, the Smith his Forge*; but this Mistake is justly exploded. . . .

[The critics say] . . . "We might give you various Instances more of the essential difference between the old Saxon and modern English Tongue, but these must satisfy any reasonable Man, that it is so great, that the Saxon can be no Rule to us; and that to understand ours, there is no need of knowing the Saxon; and tho' Dr. Hickes must be allow'd to have been a very curious Enquirer into those obsolete Tongues, now out of use, and containing nothing valuable, yet it does by no means follow . . . that we are obliged to derive the Sense, Construction, or Nature of our present Language from his Discoveries. . . ."

What they say, that it cannot be a Rule to them, is true; for nothing can be a Rule of Direction to any Man, the use whereof he does not understand; but if to understand the Original and Etymology of the Words of any Language, be needful towards knowing the Propriety of any Language, a thing which I have never heard hath yet been denied: then do these Gentlemen stand self-condemned, there being no less than four Words, [Smith, Word, Son, Good] in the Scheme of Declensions they have borrowed from Dr. Hickes, now in use, which are of pure Saxon Original and consequently essential to the modern English. . . .

The want of knowing the Northern Languages, has occasion'd an unkind Prejudice towards them: which some have introduc'd out of Rashness, others have taken upon Tradition. As if those Languages were made up of nothing else but Monosyllables, and harsh sounding Consonants; than which nothing can be a greater Mistake. I can speak for the Saxon, Gothick, and Francick, or old Teutonick: which for aptness of compounded, and well sounding Words, and variety of Numbers, are by those learned Men that understand them, thought scarce inferior to the Greek itself. . . . I never perceiv'd in the Consonants any Hardness, but such as was necessary to afford Strength, like the Bones in a human Body, which yield it Firmness and Support. So that the worst that can be said on this occasion of our Forefathers is, that they spoke as they fought, like Men. . . .

And first I must assert, that the ancient Northern Languages, do not wholly nor mostly consist of Monosyllables. . . . It must be confest that in the Saxon, there are many Primitive Words of one Syllable, and this to those who know the Esteem that is due to Simplicity and Plainness, in any Language, will rather be judged a Virtue than a Vice: That is, that the first Notions of things should be exprest in the plainest and simplest manner, and in the least compass: and the Qualities and Relations, by suitable Additions, and Composition of Primitive Words; for which the Saxon Language is very remarkable. . . .

The Rudiments of Grammar for the English-Saxon Tongue (1715). Preface, pp. iv ff.

Elizabeth Elstob (1683–1756)

[The ornamental and useful nature of monosyllables is argued in some dozen pages of quotations, with comment, from Homer, Virgil and English poets from Chaucer to Lady Winchilsea.]

[The Anglo-Saxon words in the *Grammar* are in 'Saxon' type, and grammatical terms in Ælfric's renderings of the Latin—e.g. *geðeodnys* for *conjunction*: *dælnimend* for *participle*: *nemnigendlic* for *nominative*. The noun substantive is divided into six declensions whose key words are *smið*; *witega*; *andʒit*; *word*; *wiln*; *sunu*. Irregulars (i.e. mutation and minor forms) follow, with notes on affixes. The weak adjective's function is thought to be one of emphasis—*godcund, divine, godcunda, very divine*. *Lufian* is the regular verb example, and the graded verbs are listed as irregular, but comprehensively given. There are a short syntax, chiefly on the use of the moods and the cases, and a collection of prepositions used in composition.

In the carefully classified list of adverbs is an interesting note on *forsooth*, which seems to be thought of as a corruption of *fulsoð*. 'This word continues still in use in the word *Forsooth*, but the Sense is misunderstood: For whereas it is only a Note of Affirmation, it is used as a word of Compliment and Respect, which we find exacted with great Niceness from their Children, by the meaner sort in and about the City of London, where they are sure to be taught to say *Forsooth Mother*, and *Forsooth Grandmother*, etc.'] *Ibid. p. 50.*

EPHRAIM CHAMBERS (d. 1740)

PUNCTUATION

There is much more difficulty in *pointing*, than people are generally aware of.—In effect, there is scarce any thing in the province of the grammarians so little fixed and ascertained as this. The rules usually laid down are impertinent, dark, and deficient; and the practice, at present, perfectly capricious, authors varying not only from one another, but from themselves too. . . .

In the general, we shall only here observe, that the comma is to distinguish nouns from nouns, verbs from verbs, and such other parts of a period as are not necessarily joined together.[1]—The semi-colon serves to suspend and sustain the period when too long: —The colon, to add some new supernumerary reason, or consequence, to what is already said: —And the period, to close the sense and construction and release the voice. *Cyclopaedia* (1728).

ISAAC WATTS (1674–1748)

SEMANTIC DIFFICULTY

[It can be shown that] words of the same language which are undoubted of the same theme or primitive, will give us but very doubtful and sorry information concerning the true sense of kindred words which spring from the same theme. [E.g. Latin *strages, stratum, stramen, stragulum, sterno*: English *honest* compared with Latin *honestus*.]

The Improvement of the Mind (1741),
(edition of 1795), Pt I, p. 318.

THE ART OF GRAMMAR

The art of grammar . . . is a distinct thing from the mere knowledge of the languages; for all mankind are taught from their infancy to speak their mother tongue, by a natural imitation of their mothers and nurses, and those who are round about them, without any knowledge of the art of grammar, and the various observations and rules that relate to it.

Grammar indeed is nothing else but rules and observations drawn from the common speech of mankind in their several languages, and it teaches us to speak and pronounce, to spell and write with propriety and exactness, according to the custom of those in every nation who are or were supposed to speak and write their own language best.

Ibid. p. 320.

[1] [Earlier s.v. *comma*, the *Cyclopaedia* has the same statement, but adds that it 'conveys no clear precise idea; for what is *to distinguish the Parts of a Period not necessarily joined together?*'

The whole statement on the capriciousness of punctuation is still left verbatim in the edition published between 1779 and 1786.]

JOHN WESLEY (1703-1791)

TONES OF VOICE AND PRONUNCIATION

But the greatest and most common Fault of all is, the speaking with a Tone. Some have a Womanish, squeaking Tone: Some a singing or canting one: Some an high, swelling, theatrical Tone, laying too much Emphasis on every Sentence: Some have an awful, solemn Tone; others an odd, whimsical, whining one, not to be exprest in Words.

To avoid all Kind of unnatural Tones, the only Rule is this, Endeavour to speak in Publick just as you do in Common Conversation. Attend to your Subject, and deliver it in the same Manner, as if you were talking of it to a Friend. This, if carefully observ'd, will correct both this and almost all other Faults of a bad Pronunciation.

For a Good Pronunciation is nothing but a natural, easy and graceful Variation of the Voice, suitable to the Nature and Importance of the Sentiments we deliver.

I wou'd likewise advise every Speaker to observe those who speak well, that he may not pronounce any Word in an improper Manner. And in Case of Doubt, let him not be ashamed to ask, How such a Word is to be pronounced: As neither to desire others that they wou'd inform him whenever they hear him pronounce any word improperly.

Directions concerning Pronunciation and Gesture
(Bristol, 1749), sect. I, 7 and v, 18.

JAMES HARRIS (1709-1780)

TENSES

A Rational Scheme of Tenses

Aorist of the Present[1]
I write

Aorist of the Past
I wrote

[1] [He supplies Greek and Latin parallels.]

Aorist of the Future
I shall write

Inceptive Present
I am going to write

Middle or extended Present
I am writing

Completive Present
I have written

Inceptive Past
I was beginning to write

Middle or extended Past
I was writing

Completive Past
I had done writing

Inceptive Future
I shall be beginning to write

Middle or extended Future
I shall be writing

Completive Future
I shall have done writing

It is not to be expected that the above Hypothesis should be justified through all instances in every Language. It fares with Tenses, as with other Affections of Speech; be the Language upon the whole ever so perfect, much must be left, in defiance of all Analogy, to the harsh laws of mere Authority and Chance. *Hermes* (1751), pp. 121–3.

James Harris (1709–1780)

PAST PARTICIPLES

The English Grammar lays down a good Rule with respect to its Participles of the Past, that they all terminate in D, T, or N. This Analogy is perhaps liable to as few Exceptions, as any. Considering how little Analogy of any kind we have in our Language, it seems wrong to annihilate the few Traces, that may be found. It would be well therefore, if all Writers, who endeavour to be accurate, would be careful to avoid a Corruption, at present so prevalent, of saying, *it was wrote*, for, *it was written*; *he was drove*, for, *he was driven*; *I have went*, for, *I have gone*, etc. in all which instances a Verb is absurdly used to supply the proper Participle, without any necessity from the want of such Word.

Ibid. pp. 185–6, n.

PARTICIPLES USED AS ADJECTIVES

. . . Participles insensibly pass . . . into Adjectives. Thus *Doctus* in Latin, and *Learned* in English lose their power as *Participles,* and mean a Person possessed of an habitual Quality. Thus *Vir eloquens* means not *a man now speaking,* but a man, *who possesses the habit of speaking,* whether he speak or no. So when we say in English, he is a *Thinking* Man, an *Understanding* Man, we mean not a person, whose mind is *in actual Energy,* but *whose mind is enriched with a larger portion of those powers.*

Ibid. pp. 187–8.

CLASSIFICATION OF ADJECTIVES

It has been observed already, and must needs be obvious to all, that Adjectives, as marking Attributes, can have no Sex. And yet their having Terminations conformable to the Sex, Number and Case of their Substantive, seems to have led Grammarians into that strange absurdity of ranging them with Nouns, and separating them from Verbs, tho' with respect to these they are perfectly homogeneous; with respect to the others, quite contrary. They are homogeneous with respect to Verbs as both sorts denote Attributes; they are heterogeneous with respect to Nouns, as never properly denoting Substances.

Ibid. p. 190.

DEGREES OF COMPARISON

Among the Attributes of Substance are reckoned Quantities, and Qualities. Thus we say, *a white Garment, a high Mountain.* Now some of these

Quantities and Qualities are capable of Intension, and Remission. Thus we say, *a Garment exceedingly white*; *a Mountain Tolerably high*, or *Moderately high*. 'Tis plain therefore that Intension and Remission are among the Attributes of such Attributes. Hence then one copious source of secondary Attributives, or Adverbs, to denote these two, that is, *Intension*, and *Remission*.

. . . [The English have] their *greatly, vastly, extremely, sufficiently, moderately, tolerably, indifferently*, etc.

Farther than this, where there are different Intensions of the same Attribute, they may be compared together. Thus if the Garment A be exceedingly White, and the Garment B be moderately White, we may say, *the Garment A is more white than the Garment B*.

In these instances the Adverb *More* not only denotes Intension, but relative Intension. Nay we stop not here. We not only denote Intension merely relative, but relative Intension, than which there is none greater. Thus we not only say the Mountain A is more high than the Mountain B, but that 'tis the most high of all Mountains. Even Verbs, properly so called as they admit simple Intensions, so they admit also these comparative ones. Thus in the following Example—*Fame he loveth more than Riches, but Virtue of all things he loveth most*—the Words *more* and *most* denote the different comparative Intensions of the Verbal Attributive, *Loveth*.

And hence the rise of Comparison, and of its different Degrees; which cannot well be more, than the two Species above mentioned, one to denote simple Excess, and one to denote Superlative. Were we indeed to introduce more degrees than these, we ought perhaps to introduce infinite, which is absurd. . . . There are infinite Degrees of *more White*, between the first simple *White*, and the Superlative, *Whitest*; the same may be said of *more Great, more Strong, more Minute*, etc. The Doctrine of Grammarians about three such Degrees, which they call the Positive, the Comparative and the Superlative, must needs be absurd; both because in their Positive there is no Comparison at all, and because their Superlative is a comparative, as much as their *Comparative* itself.

Ibid. pp. 195–8.

TEMPORAL ADVERBS

Should it be asked—why *Adverbs of Time*, when Verbs have *Tenses*? The Answer is, tho' Tenses may be sufficient to denote the greater Distinctions of Time, yet to denote them all by Tenses would be a perplexity without end. What a variety of Forms, to denote *Yesterday*, *To-day*, *Tomorrow*, *Formerly*, *Lately*, *Just now*, *Now*, *Immediately*, *Presently*, *Soon*, *Hereafter*, etc.?

Ibid. p. 204.

CONNECTIVES

'Tis somewhat surprizing that the politest and most elegant of the Attic Writers, and Plato above all the rest, should have their Works filled with Particles of all kinds, and with Conjunctions in particular; while in the modern polite Works, as well of our selves as of our neighbours, scarce such a Word as a Particle, or Conjunction is to be found. Is it, that where there is a Connection in the Meaning, there must be Words had to connect; but that where the Connection is little or none, such Connectives are of little use? That Houses of Cards, without Cement, may well answer their end, but not those Houses, where one would chuse to dwell? Is this the Cause? or have we attained an Elegance, to the Antients unknown?

Ibid. pp. 259–60, n.

REASONS FOR GRAMMATICAL CONCORD

Some things co-alesce and unite of themselves; others refuse to do so without help, and as it were compulsion.... For example; all Quantities, and Qualities co-alesce immediately with their Substances. Thus 'tis we say, *a fierce Lion*, *a vast Mountain*; and from this Natural concord of Subject and Accident, arises the Grammatical Concord of Substantive and Adjective. In like manner Actions co-alesce with their Agents, and Passions with their Patients. Thus 'tis we say, *Alexander conquers*; *Darius is conquered*. Nay, as every Energy is a kind of Medium between its Agent and Patient, the whole three, Agent, Energy, and Patient, co-alesce with the same facility; as when we say, *Alexander conquers Darius*. And hence, from these Modes of natural Co-alescence, arises the Grammatical Regimen of the Verb by its Nominative, and of the Accusative by its Verb.

Ibid. pp. 262–3.

PREPOSITIONS, LITERAL AND FIGURATIVE

BUT tho' the original use of Prepositions was to denote the Relations of Place, they could not be confined to this Office only. They by degrees extended themselves to Subjects incorporeal, and came to denote Rela-

81

tions, as well *intellectual*, as *local*. Thus because in Place, he who is above, has commonly the advantage over him who is *below*, hence we transfer *over* and *under* to Dominion and Obedience; of a King we say, *he ruled over his People*; of a common soldier, *he served under such a General*. So too we say, *with* Thought; *without* Attention; thinking *over* a Subject; *under* Anxiety; *from* Fear; *out of* Love; *through* Jealousy, etc. All which instances, with many others of like kind, shew that the first Words of Men, like their first Ideas, had an immediate reference to sensible Objects, and that in after Days, when they began to discern with their Intellect, they took those Words, which they found already made, and transferred them by metaphor to intellectual Conceptions. There is indeed no Method to express new Ideas, but either this of Metaphor, or that of Coining new Words, both of which have been practised by Philosophers and wise Men, according to the nature, and exigence of the occasion.   *Ibid.* pp. 268–9.

CASE

. . . whatever we may be told of Cases in modern Languages, there are in fact no such things; but their force and power is exprest by two Methods, either by Situation, or by Prepositions; the Nominative and Accusative Cases by Situation; the rest, by Prepositions.

Ibid. pp. 273–4.

There are no Cases in the modern Languages, except a few among the primitive Pronouns, such as I and ME; JE and MOY; and the English Genitive, formed by the addition of s, as when from *Lion*, we form *Lion's*; from *Ship*, *Ship's*. From this defect however we may be enabled to discover in some instances what a case is, the Periphrasis, which supplies its place, being the Case (as it were) unfolded.   *Ibid.* p. 275.

The Accusative is that case, which to an efficient Nominative and a Verb of Action subjoins either the Effect or the passive Subject.

Ibid. p. 283.

. . . the Genitive [is] formed to express all Relations, commencing from itself; the Dative, all Relations tending to itself.   *Ibid.* p. 285.

James Harris (1709–1780)

LANGUAGE AND CIVILIZATION

[We] shall be led to observe, how Nations, like single Men, have their peculiar Ideas; how these peculiar Ideas become the Genius of their Language, since the Symbol must of course correspond to its Archetype; how the wisest Nations, having the most and best Ideas, will consequently have the best and most copious Languages; how others, whose Languages are motley and compounded, and who have borrowed from different countrys different Arts and Practices, discover by Words, to whom they are indebted for Things.

To illustrate what has been said, by a few examples. We Britons in our time have been remarkable borrowers, as our multiform Language may sufficiently shew. Our Terms in polite Literature prove, that this came from Greece; our Terms in Music and Painting, that these came from Italy; our Phrases in Cookery and War, that we learnt these from the French; and our Phrases in Navigation, that we were taught by the Flemings and Low Dutch. These many and very different sources of our Language may be the cause, why it is so deficient in Regularity and Analogy. Yet we have this advantage to compensate the defect, that what we want in Elegance, we gain in Copiousness, in which last respect few Languages will be found superior to our own. *Ibid.* pp. 407-9.

MONOSYLLABLES AND PHRASAL VERBS

It has been called a fault in our Language, that it abounds in Monosyllables. As these, in too lengthened a suite, disgrace a Composition; Lord Shaftesbury, (who studied purity of Stile with great attention) limited their number to nine, and was careful, in his *Characteristics*, to conform to his own Law. Even in Latin too many of them were condemned by Quinctilian.

Above all, care should be had, that a Sentence end not with a crowd of them, those especially of the vulgar, untunable sort, such as, *to set it up, to get by and by at it*, etc. for these disgrace a Sentence that may be otherwise laudable, and are like the Rabble at the close of some pompous Cavalcade. *Philological Inquiries in Three Parts* (1781), pp. 105-6.

VARIETIES OF DICTION

As every Sentiment must be exprest by Words; the Theory of Sentiment naturally leads to that of Diction. Indeed the Connection between them is so intimate, that the same Sentiment, where the Diction differs, is as different in appearance, as the same person, drest like a Peasant, or drest like a Gentleman. . . .

But this perhaps will be better understood by an Example. Take then the following[1]—Don't let a lucky Hit slip; if you do, be-like you mayn't any more get at it. The Sentiment (we must confess) is exprest clearly, but the Diction surely is rather vulgar and low. Take it another way— Opportune Moments are few and fleeting; seize them with avidity, or your Progression will be impeded. Here the Diction, tho' not low, is rather obscure. The Words are unusual, pedantic, and affected. But what says Shakspeare?—

> There is a Tide in the affairs of men,
> Which, taken at the flood, leads on to fortune;
> Omitted, all the Voyage of their life
> Is bound in shallows—

Ibid. pp. 184–5.

INAPPROPRIATE METAPHOR

[Harris quotes] that pleasant fellow, who speaking of an old Lady, whom he had affronted, gave us in one short Sentence no less than three choice Metaphors. I perceive (said he) her Back is up;—I must curry favour— or the Fat will be in the fire.

Nor can we omit that the same Word, when transferred to different subjects, produces Metaphors very different, as to Propriety or Impropriety.

'Tis with Propriety that we transfer the word *To Embrace*, from the Human Beings to things purely Ideal. The Metaphor appears just, when we say *To Embrace a Proposition*; *To Embrace an Offer*; *To Embrace an Opportunity*. Its Application perhaps was not quite so elegant when the old Steward wrote to his Lord, upon the subject of his Farm, that "if he met any Oxen, he would not fail to Embrace them."

Ibid. pp. 195–6.

NATURALIZED METAPHOR

There are Metaphors so obvious, and of course so naturalized, that ceasing to be Metaphors, they are become (as it were) the proper Words. 'Tis after this manner we say, a *sharp* fellow; a *great* Orator; the *Foot* of

---

[1] [Examples italicized in original.]

a Mountain; the *Eye* of a Needle; the *Bed* of a River; to *ruminate*, to *ponder*, to *edify*, etc. etc. *Ibid.* p. 198.

We say no more of Metaphors, but that 'tis a general Caution with regard to every Species, not to mix them, and that more particularly, if taken from subjects, which are Contrary.

Such was the Case of that Orator, who once asserted in his Oration, that—"If Cold Water were thrown upon a certain Measure, it would kindle a Flame, that would obscure the Lustre, etc., etc."

Ibid. pp. 199–200.

ARTHUR MURPHY (1727–1805)

A PLEA FOR PLAIN ENGLISH

To think clearly . . . is the original Source of good Writing, and he who considers things with Perspicuity, will also aim at the same in conveying his Sentiments to others. This is the main Use of Language, and on this Account a good Writer will avoid all Affectation of Glittering, all false ambitious Ornaments, all Prettinesses, all Conceits, quaint Turns, Points and Antitheses, which never can give Strength to an Argument, and only serve to enervate and corrupt the Imagination. As no Language can possibly have a Competency of Terms appropriated to every different Idea, Recourse was had to the Metaphor; which consists in transferring the Name of one Object to another, on Account of some Resemblance subsisting between them; but by this, in the Nature of Things, it could never be intended that an whole Piece should be carried on in a String of borrowed Phrases. . . .

I believe the late Dean Swift understood the true genuine Beauties of Writing as well as any Author, antient or modern, and I would advise the Reader to open any Part of his Works, and try whether he can find any Thing of this florid Manner, that at present serves to *elevate and surprize*. I am convinced that no Man of common Apprehension need ever read a Sentence twice over in any of this Writer's Productions; his Method is perspicuous, and at the same time elegant, without false Embellishments, and his Metaphors all bearing a palpable Allusion to the Thing they are introduced to signify. This is a Point which should always be considered. . . . Whenever I find a Person erring on this Head, he appears to me in the Light of a Child, who has blown a Bubble

85

prettily variegated and pleasing to his Fancy, and then follows it in order to keep up the Illusion as long as he can . . . in the Eye of a just Critic nothing can be more blameable than a Luxury of Words. . . .

Add to this, that all tedious Circumlocution should be quite exploded. . . . *Gray's Inn Journal* (16 December 1752).

EPHEMERAL WORDS
To Charles Ranger, Esq.

Sir,

The Languages of all Nations have ever been in a State of Fluctuation, and we find this Complaint is constantly made by the sensible and judicious in every Age. Though the Diction of the Romans is likely to endure as long as Time shall subsist; yet we find that Horace . . . is aware of the Decay of Words and Phrases, which die away, and are constantly succeeded by a sudden Birth of new Terms and Modes of Phraseology. . . . They fall, says he, like Leaves, and are replaced by a new Product; like young Persons, they flourish for a short Time, and then tend to Oblivion. The Comparison is . . . very just; and as young Men in their Bloom and Vigour are said to be *upon Town*, it is the same with Words; they are also *upon Town* for a Time, and then totally perish. I have often thought, that a weekly Bill of Words would not be unentertaining to Men of Letters, and if there was a proper Register-Office for the Purpose, where their several Births and Burials might be recorded with Accuracy and Precision, I should imagine it would furnish no disagreeable History. A Distinction might be made between a Kind of Sex in Words, according as they are appropriated to Men or Women; as for Instance, *D—n my Blood* is of male Extraction, and *Pshaw, Fiddlestick,* I take to be female. . . .

If . . . a list should be furnished of the several Terms that are born, or that die away, with a short Account of the Life and Character of each Phrase, whether it be born of honest Parents in England or Ireland, what Company it kept, whether it was Whig or Tory, Popish or Protestant, it would in my Opinion be an agreeable Addition to this verbal History. There might further be added an Account of such Expressions as might happen to be naturalized, with the Objections of the Learned, who should think proper to protest against such a Naturalization of Foreigners among the Natives of this Land. Such a Procedure could not fail to yield Satisfaction to the curious; and though it would not prevent the Instability of our Language, it would at least display the gradual Steps towards Improvement or final Destruction. For my Part, I have ever looked upon the Permanency of our Language to be of greater Consequence than the Stocks, of whatever Denomination, and for that Reason, I should be glad that some Means were devised to hinder the Diction of our Shakespear and Milton from being obliterated, and to suspend the Evils which Mr. Pope threatens us with, when he says

> And such as Chaucer is, shall Dryden be.

The Dictionary which the Erudition of Mr. Johnson is preparing for the public, may in some Measure answer this End, and, in Aid to that Design I have been, for some Time past planning a Dictionary of such Words, as appeared to me from a Concurrence of various Causes, to be most likely to be totally forgot.

[Satirical definitions follow of Creature, Thing, Patriot, Honest, Good-nature, Religion, Humbug, Worth, Party, Tragedy, Comedy, Damned, Drum, Friendship, God, Modesty, Earthquake, Fashion, Nature, Rout, Soul, Immense, Virtue, Pity: e.g.]

CREATURE, A Term to shew our Contempt of any Person whom we dislike, chiefly used by the Ladies.

WORTH, originally it meant laudable Qualities of the Mind; at present tis solely confined to a Man's Fortune. . . .

PARTY, formerly signified Divisions in the State, at present it means a Jaunt to Vaux-hall, Bedlam, Church, or any Place of Diversion.

DAMNED, When Priestcraft prevailed in this Country the People were frightened with strange Ideas of Hell. . . . At present it signifies the highest Praise we can confer. Thus we say, "A damned fine Woman; a damned charming Creature . . . etc."

DRUM, an Instrument of warlike Music used at the March of an Army, or in Time of Battle to animate the Soldiery: Hence stiled by Shakespear *the spirit-stirring Drum*. It has not been used to any Purpose by the English since the Days of the Duke of Marlborough. In its metaphorical Sense it means a Party of Cards. (Vide Rout).

MODESTY, alludes to some Custom among the antient British Ladies.

NATURE, Nothing at all; it is often called *Plastic Nature*, *universal Nature*, &c. but the Idea is always the same.

Ibid. (29 June 1754).

EDWARD MOORE (1712–1757)

GRAMMAR AND PEDANTRY

Sir,

I CANNOT help being offended at your want of correctness in a paper, which, in other respects, deserves approbation. In Number I. you say WARN *men to goodness*. The verb *warn* is unwarrantable in this place: we are warned *by* or *from*, but not *to*—The word should be *incite*. . . . In Number III . . . you have the colloquial barbarism of doing a thing *by* a man, instead of *to*. I cannot express how much I am hurt at so vulgar an impropriety. . . . I am willing to hope that these gross mistakes are only owing to inadvertency. If so, I rest

Your admirer,
Philologos.

To Philologos.

Sir,

I SHALL be very careful of mistakes for the future; and do assure you, upon my veracity, that they have hitherto proceeded from nothing but inadvertency. I am, SIR,

Your obliged servant,
A. Fitz-Adam

To Adam Fitz-Adam, Esq.

Dear Fitz,

Lord **** and I laid hold of a d—d prig of a university fellow yesterday, and carried him to our club; where, when the claret began to mount, your paper of the *World* happened to come upon the tapis. "That same Mr Fitz-Adam, says he, is a very inaccurate writer; peradventure I shall take an opportunity of telling him so in a short time." But, dear Fitz, if the prig should really send you a letter, smoke the parson, and be witty. Your inaccuracies, as he calls them, are the characteristics of a polite writer: by these alone our club is sure that you are a man of fashion. Away with pedantry and the grammar! Write like a gentleman, and with Pope, in his essay upon critics,

Snatch a grace beyond the reach of nature

Yours,
A.B.

88

To Mr. A.B.

Sir,

IN compliance with your advice, I shall avoid the pedantry of grammar, and be perfectly the gentleman in my future essays.

I am,

Your most obedient,

A. Fitz-Adam.

The World (29 March 1753).

PHILIP DORMER STANHOPE,
4th EARL OF CHESTERFIELD (1694–1773)

WORD MAGIC

The uninformed herd of mankind are governed by words and names, which they implicitly receive, without either knowing or asking their meaning. Even the philosophical and religious controversies, for the last three or four thousand[1] years, have turned much more upon words and names, unascertained and misunderstood, than upon things fairly stated. The polite world, to save time and trouble, receive, adapt, and use words, in the signification of the day; not having leisure nor inclinations to examine and analise them: and thus often misled by sounds, and not always secured by sense, they are hurried into fatal errors, which they do not give their understandings fair play enough to prevent.

In explaining words, therefore, and bringing them back to their true signification, one may sometimes happen to expose and explode those errors which the abuse of them both occasions and protects.

Ibid. (6 December 1753).

MISAPPLIED TERMS

A gentleman, is every man, who, with a tolerable suit of cloaths, a sword by his side, and a watch and snuff-box in his pockets, asserts himself to be a gentleman, swears with energy that he will be treated as such, and that he will cut the throat of any man who presumes to say the contrary.

Ibid.

[1] [Edition of 1776, 'hundred'.]

English Examined

I heard the other day with great pleasure from my worthy friend Mr Dodsley, that Mr Johnson's English dictionary, with a grammar and history of our language prefixed, will be published this winter, in two large volumes in folio.

I had long lamented that we had no lawful standard of our language set up, for those to repair to, who might chuse to speak and write it grammatically and correctly; and I have as long wished that either some one person of distinguished abilities would undertake the work singly, or that a certain number of gentlemen would form themselves, or be formed by the government, into a society for that purpose. The late ingenious doctor Swift proposed a plan of this nature to his friend (as he thought him) the lord treasurer Oxford, but without success; . . . [If the work can be done by one man, Mr Johnson] . . . will bring this as near to perfection as any one man could do. The plan of it, which he published some years ago, seems to me to be a proof of it. Nothing can be more rationally imagined, or more accurately and elegantly expressed. . . .

I cannot help thinking it a sort of disgrace to our nation, that hitherto we have had no such standard of our language [as the Dictionaries of Italy, France, and Spain]; our dictionaries at present being more properly what our neighbours the Dutch and Germans call theirs, Word-books, than dictionaries, in the superior sense of that title. All words, good and bad, are there jumbled indiscriminately together, insomuch that the injudicious reader may speak and write as inelegantly, improperly, and vulgarly as he pleases, by and with the authority of one or other of our word-books.

It must be owned that our language is at present in a state of anarchy; and hitherto, perhaps, it may not have been the worse for it. During our free and open trade, many words and expressions have been imported, adopted and naturalized, from other languages, which have greatly enriched our own. Let it still preserve what real strength and beauty it may have borrowed from others, but let it not, like the Tarpeian maid, be overwhelmed and crushed by unnecessary foreign ornaments. The time for discrimination seems to be now come. Toleration, adoption and naturalization, have run their lengths. Good order and authority are now necessary. But where shall we find them, and at the same time, the obedience due to them? We must have recourse to the old Roman expedient in times of confusion, and chuse a dictator. Upon this principle I give my vote for Mr Johnson to fill that great and arduous post. And I hereby declare that I make a total surrender of all my rights and privileges in the English language, as a free-born British subject, to the said Mr Johnson, during the term of his dictatorship. Nay more; I will not only obey him, like an old Roman, as my dictator, but, like a modern Roman, I will implicitly believe in him as my pope, and hold him to be infallible while in the chair; but no longer.

Ibid. (28 November 1754).

THE SPREAD OF ENGLISH

I confess that I have so much honest English pride, or perhaps, prejudice, about me, as to think myself more considerable for whatever contributes to the honour, the advantage, or the ornament, of my native country. I have therefore a sensible pleasure in reflecting upon the rapid progress which our language has lately made, and still continues to make, all over Europe. It is frequently spoken, and almost universally understood, in Holland; it is kindly entertained as a relation in the most civilized parts of Germany; and it is studied as a learned language, though yet little spoke, by all those in France and Italy who either have, or pretend to have, any learning.

[French spread over 'most parts of Europe' as a result of Louis XIV's conquests, aided by 'most excellent authors', whereas] our language has made it's way singly by it's own weight and merit, under the conduct of those leaders, Shakespeare, Bacon, Milton, Locke, Newton, Swift, Pope, Addison, etc. A nobler sort of conquest, and a far more glorious triumph, since graced by none but willing captives!

These authors, though for the most part but indifferently translated into foreign languages, gave other nations a sample of the British genius. The copies, imperfect as they were, pleased, and excited a general desire of seeing the originals; and both our authors and our language soon became classical.

But a grammar, a dictionary, and a history of our language through its several stages, were still wanting at home, and importunately called for from abroad. Mr Johnson's labours will now, and, I dare say, very fully, supply that want, and greatly contribute to the farther spreading of our language in other countries. Learners were discouraged by finding no standard to resort to, and, consequently, thought it incapable of any: they will now be undeceived and encouraged. *Ibid.*

VOGUE WORDS

Not content with enriching our language by words absolutely new,[1] my fair countrywomen have gone still farther, and improved it by the application and extension of old ones to various and very different significations. They take a word and change it, like a guinea, into shillings for pocket money, to be employed in the several occasional purposes of the day. For instance, the adjective *vast*, and it's[2] adverb *vastly*, mean anything, and are the fashionable words of the most fashionable people. A fine woman (under this head I comprehend all fine gentlemen too, not knowing in truth where else to place them properly) is *vastly* obliged, or *vastly* offended, *vastly* glad, or *vastly* sorry. Large objects are *vastly* great, small ones are *vastly* little; and I had lately the pleasure to hear a fine woman pronounce, by a happy metonymy, a very small gold snuff-box that was produced in company to be *vastly* pretty, because it was *vastly* little. Mr. Johnson[3] will do well to consider seriously, to what degree he will restrain the various and extensive significations of this great word.   *Ibid.* (5 December 1754).

SPELLING, CONVENTIONAL AND PHONETIC

We have at present two very different orthographies, the PEDANTIC, and the POLITE: the one founded upon certain dry and crabbed rules of etymology and grammar, the other singly upon the justness and delicacy of the ear. I am thoroughly persuaded that Mr. Johnson will endeavour to establish the former; and I perfectly agree with him, provided it can be quietly brought about. Spelling, as well as music, is better performed by book than merely by the ear, which may be variously affected by the same sounds. I therefore most earnestly recommend to my fair countrywomen, and to their faithful or faithless servants, the

[1] I assisted at the birth of that most significant word *Flirtation*, which dropped from the most beautiful mouth in the world, and which has since received the sanction of our most accurate Laureat in one of his comedies. [*O.E.D.'s* first example in the modern sense is from 1718.]

[2] [its in 1776 edition.]

[3] [Mr Johnson's definitions:
   VAST: 1. Large; great
              2. Viciously great; enormously extensive or capacious
   VASTLY: Greatly; to a great degree.]

fine gentlemen of this realm, to surrender, as well for their own private as for the public utility, all their natural rights and privileges of misspelling, which they have so long enjoyed, and so vigorously exerted.

Ibid.

RICHARD OWEN CAMBRIDGE (1717–1802)

FASHIONABLE JARGON

I must . . . beg leave . . . to doubt the propriety of joining to the fixed and permanent standard of our language a vocabulary of words which perish and are forgot within the compass of the year.

That we are obliged to the ladies for most of these ornaments to our language, I readily acknowledge. . . . From hence only can we account for that jargon which the French call the *Bon ton*, which they are obliged to change continually, as soon as they find it prophaned by any other company but one step lower than themselves in their degrees of politeness. . . .

In order therefore to interpret every new word, and what is still more important, to give the different acceptations of the same words, according to the various senses in which they are received and understood in the different parts of this extensive metropolis, I would recommend a small portable vocabulary to be annually published and bound up with the almanack. . . .

I remember when a certain person informed a large company at the polite end of the town, that, in the City, a *Good Man* was a term meant to denote a man who was able and ready at all times to pay a bill at sight, the whole assembly shook their heads, and thought it was a strange perversion of language. . . . *Odd Man* is a term we frequently hear vociferated in the streets, when a chairman is in want of a partner. But when a lady of quality orders her porter to let in no *Odd People*, she means all decent grave men, and women who have never been talked of, many of her own relations, and all her husband's.

Besides those words which owe their rise to caprice or accident, there are many which, having been long confined to particular professions, offices, districts, climates, etc. are brought into public use by fashion, or the reigning topic on which conversation has happened to dwell for

any considerable time.[1] During the great rebellion they talked universally the language of the scriptures. "To your tents, O! Israel",[2] was the
well-known cry of Faction in the streets. They beat the enemy *from
Dan even unto Beersheba*, and expressed themselves in a manner which
must have been totally unintelligible except in those extraordinary
times, when people of all sorts happened to read the Bible. To these
succeeded the Wits of Charles's days; to understand whom it was necessary to have remembered a great deal of bad poetry; as they generally
began or concluded their discourse with a couplet. In our own memory
the late war, which began at sea, filled our mouths with terms from that
element. The land war not only enlarged the size of our swords and hats,
but of our words also. The peace taught us the language of the secretary's
office. Our country squires made *treaties* about their game, and ladies
negotiated the meeting of their lap-dogs. Parliamentary language has
been used without doors. We drink claret or port according to the state
of our *finances*. To spend a week in the country or town is a *measure*;
and if we dislike the *measure*, we put a *negative* upon it. With the rails
and buildings of the Chinese, we adopted also for a while their language.
A doll of that country, we called a Joss, and a slight building a pagoda.
For that year we talked of nothing but palanquins, nabobs, mandar-
ins, junks, sipoys, etc. To what was this owing but the war in the East
Indies?

I would therefore farther propose, in order to render this work compleat, that a supplement be added to it, which shall be an explanation
of the words, figures, and forms of speech of the country that will most
probably be the subject of conversation for the ensuing year.... I wish
such a work had been published time enough to have assisted me in
reading the following extract of a letter from one of our colonies.

—"The Chippoways and Orundaks are still very troublesome. Last
week they *scalped* one of our Indians; but the *six nations* continue firm;
and at a meeting of *Sachems* it was determined *to take up the hatchet*, and

[1] [Cf. Johnson's Life of Waller:
'Cromwell, now Protector, received Waller, as his Kinsman, to familiar conversation. Waller, as he used to relate, found him sufficiently versed in ancient
history; and when any of his enthusiastic friends came to advise or consult him,
could sometimes overhear him discoursing in the cant of the times: but when
returned, he would say, "Cousin Waller, I must talk to these men in their own
way:" and resumed the common style of conversation.'—*The Lives of the most
eminent English Poets*, edition of 1793, vol. 1, p. 211.]
[2] [I have substituted inverted commas for the italics of the original.]

make the war-kettle boil. The French desired *to smoak the calumet of peace*; but the *half-king* would not consent. They offered the *speech-belt*, but it was refused. Our governour has received an account of their proceedings, together with *a string of wampum*, and *a bundle of skins to brighten the chain*".... *Ibid.* (12 December 1754).

GEORGE JEFFREYS (1678–1755)

IN DEFENCE OF MONOSYLLABLES

What I have to offer . . . may be called a vindication of our language, and of our best poets, who have authorised the use of monosyllable lines by frequent examples of them, not out of choice, but because they could not avoid them, between the multitude of English monosyllables, and the restraint of rhyme and measure. Pope, in his *Essay on Criticism*, exposes monosyllable verses, that are rough; but there, and in his other poems, he is free enough in the use of those that are smooth; and so are Dryden, Waller, Prior, etc. . . .

As far, therefore, as the constant practice of our most celebrated poets can be of weight, monosyllable verses are justified; and to prove that they deserve to be so, instead of being only excused, as slips and defects incident to the best writers, I shall admit what a certain author says, that "verses ought to run like Ovid's, or walk like Virgil's, and not to stand stock still like doctor Donne's;" if therefore monosyllabic lines, under proper management can both "walk" and "run", when occasion requires them so to do, nothing better can be expected from polysyllables, by those who are fondest of them: and this will always be the case, when "well-vowelled words" (as Dryden calls them) are chosen, and where there is a convenient mixture of liquids and short syllables, though long ones will, now and then, serve the turn, if they open upon one another more or less, by beginning or ending with vowels . . . the prejudice against them [monosyllables] is grounded upon the practice of our antiquated poets, who, having little help from the Latin, dealt frequently in Teutonic monosyllables, and those generally rough; and hence arose the consequence *ab abusu non ad usum,* from rough monosyllables, to monosyllables as such, though ever so smooth, and from the many which occur in our old English, to the very few that are required in the course of our modern versification, upon any subject whatsoever; but were they many more, and not offensive to the ear, it is hard to say, why they should be censured.

From *Letters by Several Eminent Persons Deceased* (1772), vol. II, pp. 315–20.

ANONYMOUS CONTRIBUTOR TO 'THE WORLD'

FEMININE VOCABULARY[1]

Such is the pomp of utterance of our present women of fashion; which, though it may tend to spoil many a pretty mouth, can never recommend an indifferent one. And hence it is that there is so great a scarcity of originals, and that the ear is such a daily sufferer from an identity of phrase, whether it be *vastly, horridly, abominably, immensely,* or *excessively,* which, with three or four more calculated for the same swiss-like service, make up the whole scale or gamut of modern female conversation.

The World (6 May 1756).

SIR JAMES MARRIOTT (1730?–1803)

THE GENTEEL MANIA

... I believe ... that we shall find the *Genteel Mania* to have a long while extended itself with the most general influence among us.

The mere word *Genteel* seems to have had so singular an efficacy in the very sound of it, as to have done more to the confounding all distinctions, and promoting a levelling principle, than the philosophic reflections of the most profound teacher of republican maxims.

To do the *genteel* thing, to wear the *genteel* thing, a *genteel* method of education and living, and a *genteel* way of becoming either a knave or a bankrupt, has ruined as many once worthy families as a plague or a civil war, and rooted out of this country more real virtues than can be replanted in it for many centuries. ...

So deeply are all ranks of people impressed with the *Genteel,* that Mrs Betty is of opinion that routs would be very *genteel* in the kitchen;

[1] [From an issue given over to a skit on the loud and overbearing tones of the ladies.]

Sir James Marriott (1730?–1803)

and it is no surprising thing for a Monmouth-street broker to assure a basket-woman that the old gown he would sell to her is *perfectly Genteel.* . . .

Florio made a good figure in the university . . . till . . . a scheme to town inspired him with the notions of *Gentility,* usually contracted at the Shakespear and a Bagnio. . . . His equipage, house and liveries, were the model of *Gentility* to men who had less genius for invention, though more fortune, than himself; till, having reduced the little patrimony left him by a frugal father, he was cured of the *Genteel* by a poor regimen in the fleet.[1]   *Ibid.* (21 October 1756).

ROBERT LOWTH (1710–1787)

DOES ENGLISH OFFEND AGAINST GRAMMAR?

[A comment on Swift's charge:] Does it mean that the English Language, as it is spoken by the politest part of the nation, and as it stands in the writings of our most approved authors, often offends against every part of Grammar? Thus far, I am afraid, the charge is true. Or does it further imply, that our language is in its nature irregular and capricious; not hitherto subject, nor easily reducible, to a System of rules? In this respect, I am persuaded, the charge is wholly without foundation.

The English Language is perhaps of all the present European Languages by much the most simple in its form and construction. Of all the ancient Languages extant That is the most simple, which is undoubtedly the most ancient; but even that Language itself does not equal the English in simplicity.

The words of the English Language are perhaps subject to fewer variations from their original form than those of any other. Its Substantives have but one variation of Case; nor have they any distinction of Gender, beside that which nature hath made. Its Adjectives admit of no change at all, except that which expresses the degrees of comparison. All the possible variations of the original form of the Verb are not above six or seven; whereas in many Languages they amount to some hundreds; and almost the whole business of Modes, Times, and Voices, is managed with great ease by the assistance of eight or nine commodious little Verbs, called from their use Auxiliaries. . . .

[1] [*Fleet* in 1776 edition. The Fleet Prison is meant.]

In truth, the easier any subject is in its own nature, the harder it is to make it more easy by explanation; and nothing is more unnecessary, and at the same time commonly more difficult, than to give a demonstration in form of a proposition almost self-evident. . . .

It is not the Language, but the practice, that is in fault. The truth is, Grammar is very much neglected among us: and it is not the difficulty of the Language, but on the contrary the simplicity and facility of it, that occasions this neglect. Were the Language less easy and simple, we should find ourselves under a necessity of studying it with more care and attention. But as it is, we take it for granted, that we have a competent knowledge and skill, and are able to acquit ourselves properly, in our native tongue. . . .

A Grammatical Study of our own Language makes no part of the ordinary method of instruction, which we pass through in our childhood; and it is very seldom that we apply ourselves to it afterwards. Yet the want of it will not be effectually supplied by any other advantages whatsoever. Much practice in the polite world, and a general acquaintance with the best authors, are good helps; but alone will hardly be sufficient: we have writers who have enjoyed these advantages in their full extent, and yet cannot be recommended as models of an accurate style. Much less then will what is commonly called Learning serve the purpose; that is, a critical knowledge of ancient authors. . . .

A Short Introduction to English Grammar: with critical notes.
(From the new corrected edition, 1785; first published 1762.)
From the Preface, pp. v–viii.

UNIVERSAL GRAMMAR

Universal Grammar cannot be taught abstractedly: it must be done with reference to some Language already known; in which the terms are to be explained, and the rules exemplified. The learner is supposed to be unacquainted with all but his native tongue; and in what other, consistently with reason and common sense, can you go about to explain it to him? When he has a competent knowledge of the main principles of Grammar in general, exemplified in his own Language, he then will apply himself with great advantage to the study of any other. To enter at once upon the Science of Grammar, and the Study of a foreign Language, is to encounter two difficulties together, each of which would be much lessened by being taken separately and in its proper order. For these plain reasons, a competent grammatical knowledge of our own Language is the true foundation, upon which all Literature, properly so called, ought to be raised. If this method were adopted in our Schools; if children were first taught the common principles of Grammar, by some short and clear System of English Grammar, which, happily by its simplicity and facility is perhaps better fitted than that of any other Language for such a purpose, they would have some notion of what they were going about, when they should enter into the Latin Grammar; and would hardly be engaged so many years, as they now are, in that most irksome and difficult part of Literature, with so much labour of the memory, and with so little assistance of the understanding.

Ibid. pp. xi–xii.

NOTE ON THE GENITIVE

"Christ his sake," in our Liturgy, is a mistake either of the Printers, or of the Compilers. "Nevertheless, Asa *his* heart was perfect with the Lord". I Kings xv, 14. "To see whether Mordecai *his* matters would stand". Esther iii. 4.

"Where is this mankind now? Who lives to age
Fit to be made Methusalem *his* page?".

Donne.

"By young Telemachus *his* blooming years"

Pope's Odyssey.

"My Paper is the *Ulysses his* bow, in which every man of wit or learning may try his strength". Addison, Guardian No. 98.

This is no slip of Mr. Addison's pen: he gives us his opinion upon this point very explicitly in another place. "The same single letter (*s*) on many occasions does the office of the whole word, and represents the *his* and *her* of our forefathers". Addison, Spect. No. 135.[1] The latter instance might have shewn him how groundless this notion is: for it is not easy to conceive, how groundless this added to a Feminine Noun should represent the word *her*; any more than it should the word *their*, added to a Plural Noun; as, "the *children's* bread". But the direct derivation of this Case from the Saxon Genitive Case is sufficient of itself to decide this matter.

[So Dr Johnson thought.]   *Ibid.* p. 20.

[1] [See p. 67 of this book. Lowth misquotes Addison's '*a* whole word'.]

MOOD IN THE VERB

A Mode is a particular form of the Verb, denoting the *manner* in which a thing is, does, or suffers; or expressing an intention of mind concerning such being, doing, or suffering. As far as Grammar is concerned, there are no more Modes in any language, than there are forms of the Verb appropriated to the denoting of such different manners of representation . . . in English the several expressions of Conditional Will, Possibility, Liberty, Obligation, etc. come all under the Subjunctive Mode. The mere expressions of Will, Possibility, Liberty, Obligation, etc., belong to the Indicative Mode: It is their Conditionality, their being subsequent, and depending upon something preceding, that determines them to the Subjunctive Mode. And in this Grammatical Modal Form, however they may differ in other respects Logically, or Metaphysically, they all agree. *Ibid.* pp. 38–9, n. 4.

'THOU' AND 'YOU'

Thou, in the Polite and even in the Familiar Style, is disused, and the Plural *You* is employed instead of it; we say, *You have*; not *thou hast*. Though in this case we apply *You* to a single Person, yet the Verb too must agree with it in the Plural Number: it must necessarily be, *You have*; not *You hast*. *You was*, the Second Person Plural of the Pronoun placed in agreement with the First or Third Person Singular of the Verb, is an enormous Solecism: and yet Authors of the first rank have inadvertently fallen into it. "Knowing that *you was* my old master's good friend." Addison, Spect. No 517. . . . "Would God *you was* within her reach." Bolingbroke to Swift, Letter 46. . . . "I am just now as well, as when *you was* here." Pope to Swift, P.S. to Letter 56. On the contrary, the Solemn Style admits not of *You* for a Single Person. This hath led Mr Pope into a great impropriety in the beginning of his Messiah:

> O *Thou* my voice inspire,
> Who *touch'd* Isaiah's hallow'd lips with fire!

The Solemnity of the Style would not admit of *You* for *Thou* in the Pronoun; nor the measure of the Verse *touchedest*, or *didst touch*, in the Verb; as it indispensably ought to be, in the one, or the other, of these two forms: *You*, who *touched*; or *Thou* who *touchedst*, or *didst touch*. . . .

In order to avoid this Grammatical inconvenience, the two distinct forms of *Thou* and *You* are often used promiscuously by our modern

Poets, in the same Poem, in the same Paragraph, and even in the same Sentence; very inelegantly and improperly:

> "Now, now, I seize, I clasp *thy* charms;
> And now *you* burst, ah cruel! from my arms".
>
> Pope.

Hath properly belongs to the serious and solemn style; *has* to the familiar. The same may be observed of *doth* and *does.*   *Ibid.* pp. 41-2, n. 5.

'SHALL' AND 'WILL'

Will, in the first Person singular and plural, promises or threatens, in the second and third Persons, only foretells: *shall*, on the contrary, in the first Person simply foretells; in the second and third Persons, promises, commands, or threatens.* But this must be understood of Explicative Sentences; for when the Sentence is Interrogative, just the reverse, for the most part, takes place: Thus, "I *shall* go; you *will* go;" express event only: but, "*will* you go?" imports intention; and "*shall* I go?" refers to the will of another. But again, "he *shall* go" and "*shall* he go?" both imply will, expressing or referring to a command. *Would* primarily denotes inclination of will; and *should*, obligation: but they both vary their import; and are often used to express simple event.

Ibid. pp. 50-1.

* This distinction was not observed formerly as to the word *shall*, which was used in the Second and Third Persons to express simply the Event. So likewise *should* was used, where we now make use of *would.* See the Vulgar Translation of the Bible.

VERB FORMS

[Lowth says, wrongly, that] loveth, turneth, are contracted into *lov'th,* *turn'th,* and these for easier pronunciation immediately become *loves, turns.* . . .

Verbs ending in *ch, ck, p, x, ll, ss,* in the Past Time Active and the Participle Perfect or Passive, admit the change of *ed* into *t*; as,* *snacht, checkt, snapt, mixt, dwelt, past.*   *Ibid.* p. 57.

* Some of these contractions are harsh and disagreeable; and it were better, if they were avoided and disused: but they prevail in common discourse, and are admitted into Poetry; which latter indeed cannot do without them.

Those that end in *ve* change also *v* into *f*; as *bereave, bereft*: *leave, left*; because likewise *v* after a short vowel will not easily coalesce with *t*.

Ibid. p. 58.

[The verb to read] in the Past Time and Participle is pronounced short, *read, red, red*; like *lead, led, led*; and perhaps ought to be written in this manner: our ancient writers spelt it *redde*.

Ibid. p. 59, n. 5.

[Lowth gives past participle *beaten* as alternative to *beat, bursten* to *burst, gat* as alternative preterite to *got: gotten* as the past participle: *holpe* as a conversational form of *helped, hoven* as past participle of *heave, crope* as preterite of *creep* (past participle *creeped* as well as *crept*): *clomb* as preterite of *climb, strucken* as well as *stricken, sitten* as past participle of *sit, spitten* of *spit, lien* of *lie* (down), *baken, folden, washen, wreathen* as past participles with regular forms for all but the last two: *slang* as preterite of *sling, clang* of *cling*.

On the general confusion of forms, Lowth admits that our choice is established by Custom 'beyond recovery' in some verbs:] in the rest it seems wholly inexcusable. The absurdity of it will be plainly perceived in the example of some of these Verbs, which Custom has not yet so perverted. We should be immediately shocked at *I have knew, I have saw, I have gave*, etc., but our ears are grown familiar with *I have wrote, I have drank, I have bore*, etc. which are altogether as barbarous.

Ibid. Section on Irregular Verbs, concluding on p. 77.

Verbs ending with a single consonant preceded by a single Vowel, and, if of more than one Syllable, having the accent on the last Syllable, double the Consonant in the Present Participle, as well as in every other part of the Verb in which a Syllable is added: as, *put, putting, putteth; forget, forgetting, forgetteth; abet, abetting, abetteth.*

Ibid. p. 78.

Some verbs having the Accent on the last Syllable but one, as, *worship, counsel*, are represented in like manner as doubling the last consonant in the formation of those parts of the Verb, in which a Syllable is added; as *worshipping, counselling*. But this I rather judge to be a fault in the spelling; which neither Analogy nor Pronunciation justifies.

Ibid. p. 78, n. 9.

The Particle *a* before Participles, in the phrases *a*-coming etc. and before Nouns, as *a*-bed . . . etc; seems to be a true and genuine Preposition, a little disguised by familiar use and quick pronunciation. Dr Wallis supposes it to be the preposition *at* [so did Dr Johnson.] I rather think it is the Preposition *on*; the sense of which answers better to the intention of these expressions. *At* has relation chiefly to *place*: *on* has a more general relation and may be applied to *action*, and many other things, as well as *place*. . . . Dr Bentley plainly supposed *a* to be the same with *on*; as appears from the following passage: "He would have a learned University make Barbarisms *a* purpose". . . . .

The phrases with *a* before a Participle are out of use in the solemn style: but still prevail in familiar discourse. They are established by long usage, and good authority: and there seems to be no reason, Why they should be utterly rejected.   *Ibid.* pp. 80-1, n. 3.

THE CASE ABSOLUTE

The Adverbs *when, while, after*, etc. being left out, the Phrase is formed with the Participle, independent on the rest of the Sentence. . . . And the Case is in English always the Nominative: as,

> "God from the mount of Sinai, whose grey top
> Shall tremble, *He descending**, will himself,
> In thunder, lightning, and loud trumpet's sound,
> Ordain them Laws."
>
>   Milton, P.L. xii. 227.
>
>   *Ibid.* p. 97

[Lowth knows Milton had put *him destroy'd* in P.L. ix, 130 and commends Bentley's "vernacular instinct" which made him see his author was wrong when his "Latin Grammar Rules were happily out of his head".]   *Ibid.* p. 98, n.

* On which place, says Dr Bentley, "The Context demands that it be,—*Him descending, Illo descendente*". But *him* is not the Ablative Case, for the English knows no such Case; nor does *him* without a Preposition on any occasion answer to the Latin Ablative *illo*. I might with better reason contend, that it ought to be "*his* descending," because it is in Greek . . . in the Genitive; and it would be as good Grammar, and as proper English. This comes of forcing the English under the rules of a foreign Language, with which it has little concern. . . .

PARTICIPLE AND VERBAL NOUN

The Participle with a Preposition before it, and still retaining its Government, answers to what is called in Latin the Gerund. . . . The Participle, with an Article before it, and the Preposition *of* after it, becomes a Substantive, expressing the action itself which the Verb signifies. . . .

This Rule arises from the nature and idiom of our Language, and from as plain a principle, as any on which it is founded: namely, that a word which has the Article before it, and the Possessive Preposition *of* after it, must be a Noun; and if a Noun, it ought to follow the Construction of a Noun, and not to have the Regimen of a Verb. It is the Participial Termination of this sort of words that is apt to deceive us, and make us treat them, as if they were of an amphibious species, partly Nouns, and partly Verbs. . . . That these Participial Words are sometimes real Nouns is undeniable; for they have a Plural Number as such: as "the *outgoings* of the morning".

Ibid. p. 102, n. 3.

ON PREPOSITIONS

The Preposition is often separated from the Relative which it governs, and joined to the Verb at the end of the Sentence, or some Member of it: as, "Horace is an author, *whom* I am much delighted *with*". . . . This is an idiom, which our language is strongly inclined to: it prevails in common conversation, and suits very well with the familiar style in writing: but the placing of the Preposition before the Relative is more graceful, as well as more perspicuous; and agrees much better with the solemn and elevated style*.

Ibid. pp. 122–3.

Verbs are often compounded of a Verb and a Preposition; as, *to uphold, to outweigh, to overlook*: and this composition sometimes gives a new sense to the Verb; as *to understand, to withdraw, to forgive*. But in English the Preposition is more frequently placed after the Verb, and separate from it like an Adverb; in which situation it is no less apt to affect the sense of it, and to give it a new meaning; and may still be considered as

* Some writers separate the Preposition from its Noun in order to connect different Prepositions with the same Noun; as, "To suppose the Zodiack and Planets to be efficient *of*, and antecedent *to*, themselves." Bentley, Serm. 6. This, whether in the familiar, or the solemn style, is always inelegant; and should never be admitted, but in forms of Law, and the like; where fulness and exactness of expression must take place of every other consideration.

belonging to the Verb, and as a part of it. As, *to cast*, is to throw: but *to cast up*, or to compute, *an account*, is quite a different thing. . . . So that the meaning of the Verb, and the propriety of the phrase, depend on the Preposition subjoined.   *Ibid.* pp. 123–4.

THOMAS PERCY (1729–1811)

A NEW KIND OF POETIC DICTION

It was the constant study of the northern SCALDS to lift their poetic style as much as possible above that of their prose. So that they had at length formed to themselves in verse a kind of new language,* in which every idea was expressed by a peculiar term, never admitted into their ordinary converse. Some of these terms are founded on their mythology, or, the fabulous history of their gods: and others on some fancied analogy or resemblance. Thus if an Islandic poet had occasion to mention a rainbow, he called it, The bridge of the gods; if gold, The tears of Freya; if poesy, The gift of Odin. The earth was indifferently termed, Odin's spouse; the daughter of night, or the vessel that floats on the ages: In like manner a battle was to be styled, The bath of blood; The storm of Odin; or the clash of bucklers: the sea, The field of pirates, or the girdle of the earth. Ice was not insignificantly named, The greatest of bridges: a ship, The horse of the waves, etc.   *Five Pieces of Runic Poetry* (1763).
                                                                From the Preface.

THOMAS SHERIDAN (1719–1788)

COUNTRY, CITY AND COURTLY SPEECH

[Bad enunciation is not thought disgraceful] BUT it is not so with regard to pronunciation; in which tho' there be as great a difference between men, as in any other article, yet this difference, is not so much between individuals, as whole bodies of men; inhabitants of different countries, and speaking one common language, without agreeing on the manner of pronouncing it. Thus not only the Scotch, Irish, and Welsh, have

---

* Called by them, after the manner of the ancient Greeks, (*Asom-maal,*) THE LANGUAGE OF THE GODS.

each their own idioms, which uniformly prevail in those countries, but almost every county in England, has its peculiar dialect. Nay in the very metropolis two different modes of pronunciation prevail, by which the inhabitants of one part of the town, are distinguished from those of the other. One is current in the city, and is called the cockney; the other at the court-end, and is called the polite pronunciation. As amongst these various dialects, one must have the preference, and become fashionable, it will of course fall to the lot of that which prevails at court, the source of fashions of all kinds. All other dialects, are sure marks, either of a provincial, rustic, pedantic, or mechanic education; and therefore have some degree of disgrace annexed to them. And as the court pronunciation is no where methodically taught, and can be acquired only by conversing with people in polite life, it is a sort of proof that a person has kept good company, and on that account is sought after by all, who wish to be considered as fashionable people, or members of the beau monde.

A Course of Lectures on Elocution (1763), Lecture II, pp. 50–1
(quoted from the second edition, Dublin, 1764).

IRISH BROGUE

... the gentlemen of Ireland ... differ from those of England, chiefly in two of the sounds belonging to the vowels a and e. The words patron, matron, for example, are pronounced by them patron, matron,[1] the *a* being sounded as it is in father; fever, sea, please, are pronounced like, favour, say, plays. They soon become conscious of this diversity of sound, and not knowing exactly in which words it is used, in order to imitate the English pronunciation, they adopt the sound ee in all words without distinction; instead of great they say greet, for occasion occeesion, days dees, etc.

Ibid. p. 52.

COCKNEY

How easy would it be to change the cockney pronunciation, by making use of a proper method! The chief difference lies in the manner of pronouncing the ve, or u consonant as it is commonly called, and the w;

[1] [This helpless statement would have been avoided if Sheridan could have used phonetic script. In the 'Prosodial Grammar' prefixed to his *Dictionary*, he distinguishes the vowels by numbers. The *a* of *father* is *a*^{1}, that of *patron* *a*^{2}, in the pronunciations given in the *Dictionary*.]

which they frequently interchangeably use for each other. Thus they call veal weal, vinegar winegar. On the other hand they call winter vinter, well vell. Tho' the converting the *w* into a *v* is not so common as the changing the *v* into a *w*.

Another vice in the cockney pronunciation is, the changing the sound of the last syllables of words ending in ow, where ever it is not sounded like a dipthong, [*sic*] but like a simple o, (which is always the case when the last syllable is unaccented) into er—as feller for fellow—beller, holler, foller, winder,—for bellow, hollow, follow, window. As also adding the letter r to all proper names ending in *a* unaccented, as Belindar, Dorindar, for Belinda, Dorinda.   *Ibid.* pp. 54 and 55.

DIALECT AND THE ASPIRATE

WITH respect to the rustic pronunciation, prevailing in the several counties, I mean amongst the gentry, and such as have a liberal education, there does not seem to be any general errour of this sort; their deviations being for the most part, only in certain words, sounded in a peculiar manner by each county; and which probably owe their present pronunciation, to the continuation of the old custom; which like other antiquated modes, changes more slowly in proportion to their distance from, or want of communication with the court. . . .

But there is one defect which more generally prevails in the counties than any other, and indeed is daily gaining ground amongst the politer part of the world. I mean the omission of the aspirate in many words by some, and in most by others. Were this custom to become general, it would deprive our tongue of one great fund of force and expression. For not only certain words have a peculiar energy, but several emotions of the mind are strongly marked, by this method of shooting out the words . . . with the full force of the breath. As in the exclamations what? when? where? why? how! hark! hist!—In the words hard, harsh, heave, hurt, whirl, whisper, whistle. If any one were to pronounce the following sentence, Hail ye high ministers of Heav'n! how happy are we in hearing these your heavenly tydings! without an aspirate thus—Ail ye igh ministers of eaven! ow appy are we in earing these your eavenly tydings! who does not see that the whole expression of triumph and exultation would be lost? And the same may be observed with regard to the opposite expression of abhorrence and detestation, if the following sentence, How I hate, how I abhor such hell-hounds! were pronounced

107

in the same manner, ow I ate, ow I abor such ell-ounds. But let no one imagine, that because he would not pronounce many successive words, or a whole sentence in this manner, he is therefore entirely free from defect in this point; for I have met with but few instances in the course of my experience, and those only in the most correct speakers, of persons who have not been guilty of omitting the aspirate from some words, or giving it too faintly to others.

Ibid. pp. 55–7.

DOUBTFUL PRONUNCIATION

There are some other[1] words also of dubious sound, such as goold or gold, wĭnd or wīnd; pronunciations of this kind have their several advocates, and there is no impropriety in using either. In cases of this nature all who have an opportunity of being informed of that pronunciation, most used by men of education at court, will have the best authority on their side; as that is indeed the only standard we can refer to, in critical cases, as well as others.

Ibid. p.57.

SPOKEN AND WRITTEN LANGUAGE

. . . it will be necessary to recollect, that we have in use two different kinds of language, which have no sort of affinity between them, but what custom has established; and which are communicated thro' different organs: the one, thro' the eye, by means of written characters; the other, thro' the ear, by means of articulate sounds and tones. But these two kinds of language are so early in life associated, that it is difficult ever after to separate them; or not to suppose that there is some kind of natural connection between them. And yet it is a matter of importance to us, always to bear in mind, that there is no sort of affinity between them, but what arises from an habitual association of ideas.

Ibid. Lecture I, pp. 23–4.

CONVENTIONAL SPELLING AND CARELESS SPEECH

But it is a disgrace to a gentleman, to be guilty of false spelling, either by omitting, changing, or adding letters contrary to custom; and yet it shall be no disgrace to omit letters, or even syllables in speaking, and to

[1] [Sheridan mentions the dispute over the accentuation of *refractory* and *concordance—ref'ractory* or *refrac'tory*, *con'cordance* or *concor'dance*. (*Ibid.* p. 57).]

huddle his words so together, as to render them utterly unintelligible. Yet surely, exactness in the latter, is a point of much more importance than in the former article, in whatever light we view it. The writing of a gentleman is submitted but to one reader at a time; who may examine it at his leisure, supply any defects of orthography, and decypher the meaning, tho' the characters be ever so irregular. But the words of one who speaks in public, whether delivered, or read from notes, may be, at one and the same time, addressed to many hundred hearers; who must lose the benefit or purposed end of the discourse, in proportion as it is indistinctly pronounced.

The reason of the unequal judgment past by mankind in this case is, that written language is taught by rule, and it is thought a shame for any one, to transgress the known rules of an art, in which he has been instructed. But spoken language is not regularly taught, but is left to chance, imitation, and early habit: and therefore like all other things left to chance, or unsettled principles, is liable to innumerable irregularities and defects.   *Ibid.* Lecture II, p. 40.

PRECISION IN VOCABULARY

[Locke had complained of the imperfections of language.] Nor had he far to seek for the source of our impropriety in the use of words, when he should reflect that the study of our own language, has never been made part of the education of our youth. Consequently the use of words is got wholly by chance, according to the company that we keep, or the books that we read. And if neither the companions with whom we converse, nor the authors whom we consult, are exact in the use of their words, I can not see how it is to be expected that we should arrive at any precision in that respect. . . . The way to have clear and precise ideas affixed to the use of words, would be to have mankind taught from their early days by proper masters, the precise meaning of all the words they use.

The rising generation, so instructed, would be uniform in the use of words, and would be able to communicate their ideas to each other, with ease and perspicuity. Nor would their understandings be clouded, in private meditation, by the mists of obscurity; nor their sentiments, when delivered in conversation, perplexed by the intanglements of verbal disputation. And this might easily be effected, if only a fourth part of that time were dedicated to the study of our own tongue, which is now wasted in acquiring a smattering in two dead languages, without proving either of use or ornament to one in a hundred so instructed.

It is true, Mr Locke, in his Essay on Education, grievously complains of our neglect of studying our mother-tongue. But he lays the fault at the wrong door, when he imputes this neglect to the masters of grammar schools, and tutors at the universities. This is not part of their province. They neither profess to teach it nor do they know how. Nothing effectual can be done, without making that a distinct branch of education, and encouraging proper masters to follow it as their sole employment, in the same way as the several masters in the other branches do.

Ibid. Introductory Discourse, pp. iv–v.

ENGLISH AS A UNIVERSITY STUDY

[In his *Heads of a Plan for the Improvement of Elocution and for Promoting the Study of the English Language*,[1] Sheridan pleads for the establishment of these studies at the universities so that young gentlemen may acquire 'a grammatical knowledge of our mother tongue, and a critical skill therein, together with the art of reading it with propriety, and reciting it publicly with judgement and grace'. English masters should be provided in schools and will be more valuable than those who teach such extras as French, dancing and fencing. There should be a Society for the encouragement of such teaching. Three results would follow:]

I The establishment of an uniformity of pronunciation throughout all his Majesty's British dominions.

II The facilitating the acquirement of a just, proper delivery, to such as shall apply to it; and the enabling all such as are to speak in public, to deliver their sentiments with due grace and force, in proportion to their talents for elocution.

Lastly, The refining, ascertaining, and establishing the English language on a durable basis. . . .

As to the first article, it can not be denied that an uniformity of pronunciation throughout Scotland, Wales, and Ireland, as well as through the several counties of England, would be a point much to be wished; as it might in a great measure contribute to destroy those odious distinctions between subjects of the same King, and members of the same community, which are ever attended with ill consequences, and which are chiefly kept alive by difference of pronunciation, and dialects; for

[1] [The last part of *A Course of Lectures.*]

these in a manner proclaim the place of a man's birth, whenever he
speaks, which otherwise could not be known by any other marks in
mixed societies. . . .
[The Press and the Church are great aids to uniformity.]

Ibid. pp. 248-9.

THE IMPORTANCE OF THE STUDY
OF THE MOTHER TONGUE

THAT it is by regular study only that we acquire knowledge of the
dead languages, and chiefly also of foreign tongues, must be allowed;
and there are few of tolerable capacity, who with due application, and
the assistance of proper rules and masters, do not arrive at even a critical
skill in those. But how few are there in this country, who can boast the
same with respect to their own language. If it be asserted on one side,
that there is no occasion for taking such pains with regard to a mother
tongue, as the knowledge of that will come of course; it may be affirmed
on the other with greater justice, that there is much more occasion to
apply closely to the study of that, than of any other; not only as it is a
matter of much more importance to us than all the other languages in
the world, but because there are many errours, prejudices, and bad
habits to be overcome in that, which is not the case in the others. For
though the use of words will come of course, yet the right use of them
will not; unless we allow that they have always the same precise meaning
annexed to them, both by the people with whom we converse, and by
the writers whose works we read. Now nothing is more notorious than
that most disputes and controversies which are carried on both in writing
and speaking, without ever coming to a conclusion, do not arise so much
from anything as a disagreement in the meaning of words, and would
for the most part speedily be put an end to, were the disputants only
obliged to define their terms. For it must be obvious enough that two
men who use the same words with any difference of meaning, can never
agree in a conclusion. Thus the neglect of studying our language would
probably be found to be the chief source of errour both in opinion and
conduct. As our knowledge of most things must depend upon our
rightly understanding the words which are their types, any misconcep-
tion of them must occasion an errour in ideas, and that of course an
errour in conduct. For as our notions and opinions are formed upon
words, and as our actions are governed by our notions and opinions,

men's conduct in life must depend more upon skill in language, than is generally imagined. Thus the study of the native tongue is a matter of more importance to society, even with regard to morals, than will at first view be conceived. *Ibid.* pp. 255–6.

ARCHIBALD CAMPBELL (1726?–1780)

AUTHORITY AND LINGUISTIC LIFE

[The book from which this is an extract is a skit on Dr Johnson's English.]

There has been much talk about correcting, improving and ascertaining a living tongue, as well in our own country, as among the French and Italians. Many great writers, and if I mistake not, Doctor Swift among the rest, have thought a Grammar and Dictionary necessary for that purpose, and have therefore lamented the want of them. . . . 'Tis certain that a Grammar or Dictionary, if good for anything, must be compiled or extracted from good authors; but that these again should become necessary, and even indispensible to form, or rather to create good authors, appears to me, I confess, something like a circle in logick, or the perpetual motion in mechanicks; the one a vicious mode of reasoning, and the other a downright impossibility. 'Tis true, they may be useful to ladies or country squires, to avoid an error in spelling, and now and then a gross blunder or impropriety in speech. And farther I conceive their utility, however boasted of, does not extend; unless, indeed, in a dead language, or to a foreigner who studies a living one, in the same manner we are obliged to study Greek or Latin. But an author or an orator, who takes upon him to write or speak to the people in their own tongue, ought to be above consulting them. [Experience and history show that] as the want of them has been no loss, so when procured, they have done as little service. Homer and Virgil, Demosthenes and Cicero, Thucydides and Livy, all wrote without Grammar or Dictionary, and most of them without so much as knowing what they were. So have all the best writers of Italy, France and England. Nor do I hear that the Dictionaries of the two former . . . have done any mighty feats . . . that they have fixed or established their respective languages, or made the writers in either a whit more elegant and correct than they would have been without them. *Lexiphanes* (second edition 1767).
From the Preface, pp. xxxii–xxxiii.

Archibald Campbell (1726?–1780)

THE IDEAL DICTIONARY

It ought to contain, in a manner, a distinct treatise on every word that is, or ever has been in use, branched out into a thousand particulars very difficult to enumerate, but almost impossible to execute. And what man or body of men are equal to such a task? Besides, were it executed, who could use it, or reap any benefit from it? It would be in itself a library.... In short, we may pronounce a perfect Dictionary to be like the Philosopher's Stone, . . . impossible to obtain, and which, perhaps, we are better without.

Ibid. pp. xxxiv–v.

[If Swift's proposal for an Academy had been successful, Johnson would have probably been elected Secretary, and then 'matters would have been much worse, and really past redemption'.]

Ibid. p. xxxvi.

CORRUPTERS OF ENGLISH

The corruptors of our tongue, in the days of Swift and Steele, were pert lively fops; they were great curtailers of words, and took a pleasure in lopping off their first and last syllables, as owls bite off the feet of mice, in order to confine and fatten them. But our modern gentry are quite the reverse of the others; they are grave, solemn, formal coxcombs, and have much more of the ass than the ape in their composition; they cannot endure an elision, are mighty fond of long-tailed worm-like words, and as they think our own language does not afford a sufficient stock of them, they import them in great quantities from the Greek and Latin.

Ibid. pp. xxxvii–xxxviii.

AN ATTACK ON DR JOHNSON'S VOCABULARY

[The Physicians try to cure Johnson of his love of hard words—or words they consider improperly used:]

Come, throw up *powers*, that villanous word *powers*, a word never used by any good writer, but now applied by our modern fribbles to every possible thing, to every thing relating to men or beast, or to things inanimate. We hear of nothing but *powers of ridicule, mental powers, intellectual powers, patron powers of literature, powers of dolorous declamation.* Instead of saying, as people did formerly, such a one is a person of talents, parts, or abilities, the word now is, he has great *powers*, and those *powers* are, according to the wares he deals in, either *theatrical, comical, tragical, poetical* or *paradoxical*. The modern Roscius cannot step upon the stage, but in the next newspapers, our ears are stunned with the *amazing theatrical powers* of our inimitable Garrick; nor M—y *exhibit* a new piece, (another of their cant words, seldom proper but in the mouth of a puppet-man, which, however, they are sure to *exhibit* on every ordinary occasion) ... but we have a discussion in the next Review on his *comick* or *tragick powers*. . . . In the next place, get up, *gaze . . . imp, prime, forms, honours* . . . then *take the lead* a vile phrase, taken from the Card or Billiard table, *Lore, Lore*, must come away next, a word of mighty request in Prologues and Epilogues to new plays. . . . In the last place, get up *gripe, growl, rouze, throbs, whine*, words all of them English, but spoiled, Mr. J—n, by your affected use of them.   *Ibid.* pp. 126 ff.

[Other words objected to are *devoid, delate, replete, succumb, discuss, torpor, frigor, vernal, diurnal, paucity, inanity, vicinity, celebrity, hilarity, repugnant, abhorrent*.]

[Campbell adds a footnote:] I must likewise take notice in this place, that I do not pretend to reject or expunge, out of the English Language, any, far less all those words, which to preserve the humour of the Dialogue, I have caused Lexiphanes to throw up. Such a thought would be highly ridiculous; for experience and the practice of the best writers have shewn us that there is no word, not even the hardest in all his Dictionary or Ramblers, but what may be proper, nay the properest at certain times, and in some circumstances. Proper words in their proper places, is the definition of a good style given by Swift. Therefore it is not the words themselves, but their affected use, and the affected phrases that I find fault with. But how to attain the one, and to avoid the other, is not to be learned from a grammar or dictionary; but by keeping good company and studying good authors.   *Ibid.* p. 127.

BENJAMIN FRANKLIN (1706–1790)

THE CASE FOR SPELLING REFORM

Dear Madam,

The objection you make to rectifying our alphabet, "that it will be attended with inconveniences and difficulties", is a natural one; for it always occurs when any reformation is proposed; whether in religion, government, laws, and even down as low as roads and wheel carriages. —The true question then, is not whether there will be no difficulties or inconveniences; but whether the difficulties may not be surmounted; and whether the conveniences will not, on the whole, be greater than the inconveniences. In this case, the difficulties are only in the beginning of the practice: when they are once overcome, the advantages are lasting. —To either you or me, who spell well in the present mode, I imagine the difficulty of changing that mode for the new, is not so great, but that we might perfectly get over it in a week's writing.—As to those who do not spell well, if the two difficulties are compared, (viz.) that of teaching them true spelling in the present mode, and that of teaching them the new alphabet and the new spelling according to it; I am confident that the latter would be by far the best. They naturally fall into the new method already, as much as the imperfection of their alphabet will admit of: their present bad spelling is only bad, because contrary to the present bad rules: under the new rules it would be good.—The difficulty of learning to spell well in the old way is so great, that few attain it; thousands and thousands writing on to old age, without ever being able to acquire it. 'Tis, besides, a difficulty continually increasing; as the sound gradually varies more and more from the spelling: and to foreigners it makes the learning to pronounce our language, as written in our books, almost impossible.

Now as to "the inconveniences" you mention.—The first is; that "all our etymologies would be lost, consequently we could not ascertain the meaning of many words."—Etymologies are at present very uncertain; but such as they are, the old books would still preserve them, and etymologists would there find them. Words in the course of time, change their meanings, as well as their spelling and pronunciation; and we do not look to etymology for their present meanings. If I should call a man a Knave and a Villain, he would hardly be satisfied with my telling him, that one of these words originally signified only a lad or servant; and the other, an under plowman or the inhabitant of a village. It is from present usage only, the meaning of words is to be determined.

Your second inconvenience is, that "the distinction between words of different meaning and similar sound would be destroyed."—That distinction is already destroyed in pronouncing them; and we rely on the sense alone of the sentence to ascertain, which of several words, similar in sound, we intend. If this is sufficient in the rapidity of discourse, it will be much more so in written sentences; which may be read leisurely; and attended to more particularly in case of difficulty, than we can attend to a past sentence, while a speaker is hurrying us along with new ones.

Your third inconvenience is, that "all the books already written would be useless."—This inconvenience would only come on gradually in a course of ages. You and I, and other living readers, would hardly forget the use of them. People would long learn to read the old writing, though they practised the new.—And the inconvenience is not greater than what has actually happened in a similar case, in Italy. Formerly its inhabitants all spoke and wrote Latin: as the language changed, the spelling followed it. It is true that at present, a mere unlearned Italian cannot read the Latin books; though they are still read and understood by many. But if the spelling had never been changed, he would now have found it much more difficult to read and write his own language; for written words would have had no relation to sounds, they would only have stood for things; so that if he would express in writing the idea he has, when he sounds the word *Vescovo*, he must use the letters *Episcopus*.— In short, whatever the difficulties and inconveniences now are, they will be more easily surmounted now, than hereafter; and some time or other, it must be done; or our writing will become the same with the Chinese, as to the difficulty of learning and using it. And it would already have been such, if we had continued the Saxon spelling and writing, used by our forefathers.

I am, my dear friend,
Yours affectionately,
B. Franklin.

London,
Craven-Street
Sept. 28, 1768.

[The original letter is in Franklin's proposed new alphabet, which attempts to distinguish voiced and voiceless sounds, length of vowels, when a digraph represents a single sound, and when a single symbol represents a diphthong or affricate. Franklin's critic is Miss M.S. of Kensington.

His transcription shows that for him *learned* had the same vowel as *man*.]   *Philosophical Miscellanies* (1779), pp. 473-8.

JAMES BURNETT, LORD MONBODDO (1714–1799)

GOTHIC

[Monboddo reverenced Gothic, but misunderstood its relation to other Germanic languages.]
There is another language, from the name of which we should expect nothing but rudeness and barbarity, and yet it is a great work of art, such as may be compared even to the Greek, and in many respects is preferable to the Latin.

The language I mean is the Gothic, the parent of all the different dialects of the Teutonic, such as the German, the Dutch, Swedish, Danish, Icelandish, and of the English among the rest. There is only one book of it extant, and that but a short one, viz. a translation of the four gospels, which is preserved in the university of Upsal in Sweden. There are also preserved some fragments of the epistle of Paul to the Romans. From these remains, small as they are, we discover that it is a complete language in itself, having its roots all of its own growth, from which it forms the rest of its words by derivation and composition: and it is copious enough to express everything in those translations by words of its own, without borrowing one from the original Greek. . . .

The Origin and Progress of Language
(Edinburgh, 1773–92), vol. I, Pt. I, bk III, ch. 9.

A PRE-VIEW OF INDO-EUROPEAN

. . . there is so great a resemblance betwixt the language presently spoken in Persia and the Teutonic, that it is impossible it can be accidental. . . .

If it could be further proved, that the Celtic, and Teutonic, or its parent the Gothic, were originally the same language, which is the opinion of M. Bullet . . . it would, I think, establish this proposition, That there was but one language antiently spoken all over the north, northeast, and west of Europe, and the northern and western parts of Asia. Now, I should think it might be discovered with pretty great certainty, whether there was any affinity betwixt the Celtic and Teutonic, by comparing the most ancient remains of the Celtic . . . with the most antient remains of the Teutonic, such as the Edda, and other old Icelandish poems, and with what is still more antient, the remains of the Gothic.

This would be a very fine field of criticism, by which I think a great discovery might be made, not only in the matter of language, but with respect to the history of mankind: for if it could be proved, that the Celtic and Teutonic languages were originally the same, it would go far to prove, that the two races of people were likewise the same originally.

Ibid. ch. 11.

ANALYTIC SYNTAX

But suppose a language, of which the art is so imperfect that it has no cases at all, no genders of substantives, neither genders nor number of adjectives, and very little expression of numbers, even in their verbs, which is the case of the English, and, for the greater part, of all the modern languages of Europe; in what manner are the words to be connected in such a language? It is evident it can only be in one or other, or both the two ways last mentioned, namely, either by separate words, or by juxtaposition of the words to be connected together; which last way, as we have elsewhere observed, is almost the only syntax of the barbarous languages; and as it is a great part of the syntax of the modern languages of Europe, so far at least it must be admitted, that these languages approach to barbarity.

Ibid. vol. II, Pt. II, bk III, ch. 1.

DISADVANTAGES OF A FIXED WORD-ORDER

It should . . . be left to the speaker to place the words, as well as to lay the emphasis, where he thinks it will best convey his sense to the hearer. And the language which lays him under a restraint in that particular is defective. [Hence the superiority of synthetic languages.]

Ibid. ch. 2.

LINGUISTIC CORRUPTION

. . . a language of art not only could not have been invented by the people, but . . . it cannot be preserved among them, without the particular care and attention of those men of art we call grammarians; whom we may despise as much as we please; but if there be not such a set of men in every country, to guard against the abuses and corruptions which popular use will necessarily introduce into every language; and if the youth of rank and fortune in the country, are not carefully instructed by such men in the principles of grammar; the language of that country, how-

ever perfect it may have been originally, will very soon become un-learned and barbarous. It is chiefly by such neglect that all the present languages of Europe are become corrupt dialects of languages that were originally good. . . .[1]
Ibid. ch. 14.

MONOSYLLABLES

In English . . . we make some few changes upon the sound of our words, as in the preterite tenses, and participles of our verbs; in place of *loved*, we say *lov'd*, a liberty which ought to be indulged to poets only, for the sake of their verse. For, by such abridgements, we add greatly to the number of monosyllables of our language, already too much crouded with them, besides making the sound of our language still more harsh, by joining together, in the same syllable, so many consonants. . . .

Ibid. vol. III, Pt. II, bk IV, ch. 2.

METAPHOR

I have also observed, that we often use metaphorical words, not by way of ornament, but for want of proper terms; as when we say the *Foot* of a hill, or of a Chair or a table, with many like expressions. And there is a set of words, I believe, in all languages, which are metaphorical, but, for want of other words, are constantly used as proper, so that the metaphor is intirely overlooked. The words I mean are those expressing the operations of mind, which are commonly translations from bodily operations. Such are the words *reflect, ponder, ruminate*, and the like.

It is, I believe, for this reason that barbarous languages are observed to be so figurative, which by many is thought to be a sign of their rich-ness; whereas I hold it to be a proof of their poverty. For, not being able to express a thing by its proper name, they are naturally driven to tell what it is like. The most perfect natural language is, therefore, that which has proper names for everything, and uses figurative words only by way of ornament.

[1] [Monboddo's footnote to the preceding:] Though we of Britain boast of being a learned nation, I doubt the English Language is not mended in our hands. Dr. Lowth, in his excellent grammar, has collected a surprising number of barbarisms and solecisms that are to be found in our most admired authors, particularly of this century. The best authors may be guilty of inaccuracies of style through hurry and inattention; but such frequent and repeated blunders could not have proceeded but from absolute ignorance of the grammatical art.

Whoever ... borrows a metaphor from a thing that he does not understand, will be apt to apply it very improperly. ... [So] a dictionary, which only gives you different significations, without distinguishing what is proper from what is figurative, is imperfect in its kind. *Ibid.* ch. 4.

THE HARSHNESS OF ENGLISH

[English is harsh, owing to its monosyllables and mute consonants, and the prevalence of aspirated *t*: it is worsened by our habit of shortening words ... e.g. *Ev'ry* for *Every*, *lov'd* for *loved*, *built* for *builded*.]

Further, the English language is altogether unmusical, unless we are pleased to call a drum a musical instrument—For it has no melody ... nor has it rhythm; for though it have some long syllables, they bear no proportion by number to the short. .... But as, by our modern pronunciation, we aggravate the defect of length in our words, so, by a faulty pronunciation, which is increasing every day, we are taking from the beauty of our accents, by drawing them too far back, even to the third syllable, and so obscuring the pronunciation of the two final syllables.—Thus a great many pronounce *Révenue*, in place of *Revénue*, where it is evident, that the two last syllables of the word are obscured by the first syllable being accented.—Again, people now generally say, *Advértisement* in place of *Advertísement*, as they formerly pronounced; by which two long syllables are sunk in the pronunciation.—Again almost every body now says *Cómmendable* in place of *comméndable.*— Nay, we endeavour to draw back the accent, even beyond the third syllable; thus we say, *Interested.*[1]—But this being impossible by the nature of things, we are obliged to lay some stress upon the last syllable, *ted.* ... §[The] poverty of our language is so great, that we often employ the same word to express both a verb, and a substantive or adjective. Now, according to the common use of the language in my younger days, the verb was distinguished from the noun by the accent being put upon the last syllable of the verb, and the first syllable of the noun. But at present, this is neglected. Thus, for example, they said formerly, *a súbject*, and *to be súbject*, but they always said *to subjéct*. Now, many people say, to *súbject*; nay I have heard *súbjected* said, though with the greatest violation to the quantity. .... *Ibid.* vol. IV, Bk I, ch. 13.

[1] [No stress-mark: presumably it should be *ínterested*.]

James Burnett, Lord Monboddo (1714–1799)

THE DEFICIENCIES OF ENGLISH

[English verbs are defective in tenses, the persons dependent in the preterite on the use of pronouns; we supply the subjunctive by auxiliaries, our terminations suffer from tedious similarity. We have no inflected forms to express voice:—we express *edificatur* by a very awkward circumlocution (i.e. *is a-building*). Nouns have no genders or cases, adjectives no number—in all inferior to the learned languages.]

As to Derivation or Etymology.—The English language not being an original language like the Greek, but a derived language, and even the third in descent from the Gothic, and both the Gothic and its immediate parent the Saxon being unknown to us, we hardly know the etymology of any word purely English.   *Ibid.* ch. 13.

DEGENERACY

... it appears to me impossible, that a man who knows but one language, the English suppose, and so can compare it with no other, should be able to know either its defects or excellencies.... [There] is a wonderful degeneracy of this greatest, and most useful art among men ... the English is not so good a language as the Saxon, nor the Saxon, or any other dialect of the Teutonick, so compleat a language as the original Gothic.

Ibid. ch. 17.

[In the time] since I was educated among English gentlemen at a foreign university about fifty years ago, I perceive a great alteration in the language, both as to the pronunciation and the sense of words.

[To show that] we can only preserve the purity of our language by keeping to the antient standard [he instances the word *ingenuity*] which is now used, even by the best authors, to signify what is clever or acute in the operations of the mind; a sense which has no connection with the signification of the Latin word, *ingenuitas*, from which it is derived.... How much Milton and Doctor Middleton have adorned their stile by using English words derived from Latin in their true classical signification, I have elsewhere observed.   *Ibid.*

CONVERSATIONAL HABITS

In my younger days, the people of fashion in England spoke with a certain gravity and dignity becoming their rank; and there was a remarkable difference in that respect betwixt the city and the court end of the town. Now, a young gentleman of the first rank talks or rather prates like a waiter in a city tavern, in such a glib, pert, flippant manner, as to me is very offensive, and indeed, sometimes not intelligible. . . . we should suit the pitch of our voice to the number of the company. . . . As to the words, they should be of common use, and not affectedly learned or *Johnsonian*,[1] as I have heard them called. . . . in general, we ought not to seem to labour to speak well. This persons are apt to do when they speak any language other than their native; and I have particularly observed it in Scotsmen who have learned to speak English after they were become men, and who, though they speak it well, may be discovered by a nice ear to speak a language that is not native to them. . . .

There is an Attic in every country, as well as there was in Greece. The Attic in England is the language of the court and of the universities. But there are many provincial dialects: And besides these, there is what may be called a professional dialect, belonging to men of certain professions; for I have observed several gentlemen of the law, and more of the clergy, who had not been much in good company, speak in a tone and manner very different from people of fashion, and which I thought not at all beautiful.

Such peculiarities ought to be avoided.   *Ibid.* Bk II, ch. 6.

DR JOHNSON AND HIS DICTIONARY

[The Dictionary] is certainly a most laborious and, I think, an useful work. But there are many works useful and even necessary, which require no genius at all; and dictionary-making, is one of these.

[Johnson, in Monboddo's opinion, was 'neither a scholar nor a man of taste', but a pedant.]   *Ibid.* vol. v, Bk I, ch. 5.

THE IMPORTANCE OF SANSCRIT

. . . there is a language still existing, and preserved among the Bramins of India, which is a richer, and in every respect a finer language than even the Greek of Homer. All the other languages of India have a great resemblance to this language, which is called the Shanscrit: But those

---

[1] [Vol. IV bears the date 1787. *O.E.D.'s* first example—from Boswell—is dated 1791.]

languages are dialects of it, and formed from it, not the Shanscrit from them. Of this, and other particulars concerning this language I have got such information from India, that . . . I shall be able clearly to prove, that the Greek is derived from the Shanscrit, which was the ancient language of Egypt, and was carried by the Egyptians into India, with their other arts, and into Greece by the colonies which they settled there.

Ibid. vol. VI, Bk II, ch. I.

ACCENTUATION

Our young orator should be taught to know the advantages and disadvantages of the language in which he is to speak. This is best known by comparing it, first, with the learned languages, and then with some modern languages, such as the French. By comparing it with the learned languages he will find it defective in many things which adorn oratorial composition, such as melody and rhythm, and that variety of arrangement of words which the more perfect grammar of those languages admits, and which gives a wonderful beauty and variety to composition in Greek and Latin. But the English has one thing in its pronunciation which the learned languages had not, and that is what we call Accent, by which the voice is raised and made louder upon one syllable of a word than upon another.

[This gives a variety unknown to French, but obscures our pronunciation] for the vehemence of our accents is such that it obscures the following syllables of the word, of which we need no other example than the word syllable itself.[1]

Ibid. Bk III, ch. 3.

[1] [A footnote to the above:]
I have reason to think that this vehemence of accentuation, which distinguishes the English language so much from the Italian, and, I believe, from every other language in Europe, was not practised formerly in England so much as it is at present; for I have been told by some gentlemen who have been in America, and particularly by one who was there many years, that the people of New England do not accent syllables with near so much violence as the people of Old England do at present; and for that reason they speak more clearly and intelligibly. The fact appears to be, that the people of New England have preserved the language they brought with them which was the language spoken in England in the days of Milton, when men both spoke and wrote better in England than they do now.

WILLIAM DRAKE (1723–1801)

ORIGINS AND AFFINITIES OF ENGLISH

[Mr Whitaker has published a book asserting] that the English tongue was radically formed of Celtick or British materials, and derived little or no assistance from the Teutonick.

[In *Archæologia*, vol. v (1779), the Rev. Mr Drake asserts the Germanic origin of English, and compares the Gothic and English versions of St John's Gospel 10, 1–15—correctly enough, apart from his idea that the *zow* of Middle English (=*ʒow*) is the same as Gothic *izwis*.[1] When confronted with Gothic and English] a man must be little sagacious in distinguishing likenesses who does not discover that the one is the natural descendant[2] of the other; their complexions, their manners, their features, are exactly similar, and I challenge the deepest enquirer into the Celtick to produce so decisive a proof of any affinity of that tongue with ours. The British, to speak plainly, has little or no resemblance to the English. Many of their terms may have gained admission among us, as from the vicinity and long intercourse we have had with that people may necessarily be imagined, but their idioms and genius are as radically and essentially different as any two languages can possibly be.

Archaeologia, vol. v (1779), pp. 316–17. (Paper read 7 November 1776.
He adds more comparisons with Gothic in 1778.)

THOMAS TYRWHITT (1730–1786)

THE ROWLEY POEMS

[This and the following three passages, including those by Milles and Warton, give the arguments for and against the authenticity of Chatterton's Rowley Poems. They provide interesting evidence of the state of knowledge of Middle English in the late eighteenth century.]

Let it be allowed, that *barbed horse* was a proper expression in the XV Century for *a horse covered with armour*, can anyone conceive that *barbed*

---

[1] [The forms are parallel: the z-spelling makes them look more alike than they are.]

[2] [The idea that English is a descendant of Gothic is a remarkably long-lived error. But Drake was on the right lines, and offers convincing proofs of the Germanic family likeness.]

hall signified *a hall in which armour was hung?* or what other sense can *barbde* have in this passage? . . .

[On Fonnes (glossed *devices*).] A *fonne* in Chaucer signifies a *fool*, and *fonnes—fools*; and Spenser uses *fon* in the same sense; nor do I believe that it ever had any other meaning. . . .

[On 'In everich eyne', 'Wythe syke an eyne'.] *Eyne*, a contraction of *eyen*, is the plural number of *eye*. It is not more probable that an ancient writer should have used the expressions here quoted than that any one now should say—*In every eyes;—with such an eyes.* . . .

[On 'Lette *thyssen* menne'.] I cannot believe that *thyssen* was ever in use as the plural number of *this*. . . . And this leads me to the capital blunder, which runs through all these poems, and would alone be sufficient to destroy their credit; I mean, the termination of *verbs in the singular number* in *n**. . . .

[On 'blake'.] Skinner has the following article: "*Blake* and *bare*, videtur ex contextu prorsus *Nuda*, fort. q.d. *Bleak and Bare*, dum enim nudi sumus, eoque aeri expositi præ frigore pallescimus. . . ."

Chatterton has caught hold of *Nuda*, which in Skinner is the exposition of *Bare*, as if it belonged to *Blake*.

> The Appendix to the third edition (1778) of Tyrwhitt's edition of *Poems, supposed to have been written at Bristol, by Thomas Rowley, and others, in the Fifteenth Century*, pp. 317–29.

TYRWHITT'S VINDICATION OF HIS VIEWS[1]

[Examples of the commentary:]

Adave—The only *similarity*, which I can discern in these instances [those given by Milles in opposition to Tyrwhitt[2]] is, that they are irregular; and in that light, they would have served as well to justify the use of *Adoff*, or *Adohte*, for the past tense of *Adawe*. In order to form any

---

* It is not surprizing that Chatterton should have been ignorant of a peculiarity of the English language, which appears to have escaped the observation of a professed editor of Chaucer. Mr Urry has very frequently lengthened *verbs in the singular number*, by adding *n* to them, without any authority, . . . even from the errors of former Editions or MSS. It might seem invidious to point out living writers of acknowledged learning, who have slipped into the same mistake in their imitations of Chaucer and Spenser.

[1] [In 1782 Tyrwhitt wrote a *Vindication* of his Appendix in which he supported the conclusion of Thomas Warton (see p. 128).]

[2] [See p. 126.]

argument from similarity, the DEAN should have stated one instance at least of a verb in *awe*, terminating its past tense in *ave*.

Barbed. The supposition of ANONYMOUS, that *barbed*, in these passages is to be deduced from *To barb*; *to trim* and *dress the beard*, or *to put it into proper form*; is ridiculous. The expression *barbed horse*, whenever it came into our language, was certainly taken from the French *cheval bardé*—[He quotes Cotgrave and Du Cange to show that the term was appropriate to horses, not halls.]

[*Blake* is glossed as *Naked*, obsolete, in Kersey. Comparison shows that Kersey's Dictionary, mistakes and all, will account for Chatterton's strange uses of words.] . . .

The Prefix a. [The Dean] forgets that his author is not charged simply with prefixing *a* to words of all sorts, but with prefixing it, *without any regard to custom or propriety*. No one ever doubted that words of all sorts, beginning with *a*, are to be found in all authors.

The question is, whether this initial *a* is usually added arbitrarily, without any authority from custom, or any change in the signification of the word. *A Vindication of the Appendix to the Poems called Rowley's* (1782).

JEREMIAH MILLES (1714–1784)

IN DEFENCE OF 'ROWLEY'

ABORNE, like many other words in [the Rowley] poems, has the A.S. prefix, which Rowley, and all our ancient poets, insert or omit at their pleasure; for there seems to be no certain rule to determine the proper or improper use of it. . . .

Burne, Burned, Bourne, and *Ybourned*, are frequently used by our ancient poets in the senses here affixed to them.

Gower describes a Coppe,
> Which stood upon a foote on highte,
> Of *borned* gold.

and of a suit of armour,
> Which *burned* was as silver.

Lidgate mentions the wayne of Apollo, as
> Of gold *ybourned* bright and fair:

And Chaucer speaks of armour
> Wrought all of *burnid* steel.

Aborne or *Yborne* is here used as a participle, with the final *d* omitted; a liberty taken by Chaucer and other poets.

ADAVE is the past tense of *Addaw*, a word of established antiquity and signification, used by our ancient poets to signify either the awaking from sleep, the rising of the sun, or the dawning of the day: So Gower says,

The day *beddaweth*;

Chaucer, in his Prologue to the Legend of Good Women,

That *daweth* me no day; . . .

and Lidgate, in his Life of our Lady, compares her to a star,

That down from Heavyn *addaweth* all our sorrowe.

Mr Warton has explained this word by two others of very different import, viz. *Affright* and *Remove*; both equally distant from the true meaning of this passage; which signifies *to shine upon, to brighten,* or *to gild our sorrow.* So Kenewalche was "the fynest dame the sun or moon *adave*," i.e. *arose* or *shone upon.* If an objection be made to the irregularity of the tense, it may be justified by many similar instances in our ancient writers, who form *gaff* from *give, droff* from *drive, groff* from *graven, thohte* from *thinchan*, with many other irregular past tenses mentioned in Manning's Saxon Grammar, prefixed to Lye's Glossary.

ASSWAIE Ella's departure from Birtha, made him *experience* or *suffer the trial* of most torturing pains: What is this but the French word *essayer*, and the English *assay, trial*? So Gower,

I fall in such *assaie.*

But Spenser comes nearer to the word,

Didst *sway* so sharp a battle (B. v. c.3. st. 22)

ASTEND, i.e. *Astound*, is probably spelt in this manner on account of the rime, such liberties being frequent with our ancient poets. So Chaucer uses *sare* for *sore*, and *sa* for *so*, and it would be endless to quote similar instances from other poets.

BARBED HALL. If there is no objection to the *Barbed Horse* in Shakespeare's Richard the Second, there can be none to that in Ælla;

Whann from the *barbed horse* in fyghte did viewe;

nor probably to

The javelin *barbed* with death 'is wynges.

Much less can that passage be objected to in Shakespeare, where Coriolanus expresses a reluctance to appear before the senate of Rome as a supplicant, with his head *bare* and *unarmed*, which had been usually covered with a helmet:

Must I go shew them my *unbarbed* sconce?

Not his *unshaven* head, as Dr Johnson has explained the word; for that would have been no unusual appearance for a Roman, in the days of Coriolanus; but (as Sir Thomas Hanmer justly calls it) *unarmed*. Can there be any impropriety, then, in applying this expression to the hall in a gentleman's country seat, which, according to the custom of that age, was hung round with all the variety of armour then in use . . .?

BLAKE, has two different significations in the two passages quoted in the Appendix, (Ælla 178, and 406). *Blake Autumn*, means *yellow* autumn; which is very properly connected with the idea of *sun-burnt*. . . . This sense of *Blake* is well known in the northern and western parts of England, where a *yellow-hammer* is called a *Blakelyng*.

But *Blake*, signifies also *pale, sallow, black*; Chaucer uses the word in almost all these senses; and Bailey explains it by *Bleak*, i.e. *open, exposed*, and therefore *cold*; and observes that *Blakefield*, in German signifies *an open field*, a *plain*, or *flat*. In the two following passages of Rowley we are to understand *Blake* in this sense;

> *Blake* standeth future doome.

i.e. my future fate is *open* and exposed to my view.

> The *Blakied* forme of kinde

signifies the *naked* and *undisguised* manners of men.

Milles's edition of *Poems, supposed to have been written at Bristol, in the fifteenth century, by Thomas Rowley, Priest, &c.* (1782), pp. 468–86.

THOMAS WARTON (1728–1790)

AGAINST THE AUTHENTICITY OF THE ROWLEY POEMS

[Warton notes the use of modern words like *Puerility, optics, Latinised*: of *piece* in the sense of play, of *success* in the good sense: of *tragedy* in reference to a play: and of *blameless tongue*, where the 'epithet, peculiarly used, is from Pope's Homer'.]

The antient language of these poems is affected and unnatural. Antiquated expressions are engrafted on present modes of speech. . . .

The conclusion must be, that he borrowed his language from glossaries and etymological English lexicons, and not from life or practice. But he borrowed without selection or discernment. He seems to have been persuaded, that no other ingredient was necessary for his fiction than old words: and careless or ignorant of the application, which required the nicest conduct and caution, he presumed he had accomplished his design, by introducing as many antient terms, and of any antiquity, as he could collect. He viewed antient language as all of one age and one district. In dictionaries of old English, he saw words detached and separated from their context: these he seized and combined with others, without considering their relative or other accidental signification. Here too, he found the peculiarities of northern and southern dialects, thrown together for general explanation: these he carelessly blended, not observing their respective local appropriations. This confusion has been increased by misspellings, proceeding either from choice, ignorance or accident, and by inflections at once ungrammatical and arbitrary. Thus has he fabricated a factitious antient diction, at once obsolete and heterogeneous, anomalous in every respect, such as never could have been in use at any era of antiquity, is not transmitted by any antient English author, and most certainly would have been almost as little understood three centuries ago, as at present. Thus has he produced such a system of language, such a discordant tissue of words of distant provinces and distant periods, as never before coexisted. Again, this motley mixture of the modes of antient language being worked into a modern ground, has compounded such a *pasticcio* of style, as is still more unexampled and extravagant.

An Enquiry into the Authenticity of the Poems attributed to Thomas Rowley (1782), pp. 42–4.

HORNE TOOKE (1736–1812)

INTERJECTIONS

Without the artful contrivances of Language, mankind would have nothing but Interjections with which to communicate, orally, any of their feelings. The neighing of a horse, the lowing of a cow, the barking of a dog, the purring of a cat, sneezing, coughing, groaning, shrieking, and every other involuntary convulsion with oral sound, have almost as good a title to be called Parts of Speech as Interjections have. . . . And indeed where will you look for the Interjection? Will you find it amongst laws, or in books of civil institutions, in history, or in any treatise of useful arts or sciences? No. You must seek for it in rhetorick and poetry, in novels, plays and romances.

Diversions of Purley (1786), vol. I, pp. 61–3
(quoted from the edition of 1829).

WHY NOT ANGLO-SAXON?

... I should undoubtedly have conformed to [Mr Dunning's wishes for 'the common English character of the Anglo-Saxon and Gothic derivations'] if I had not imagined that, by inserting the Anglo-Saxon and Gothic characters in this place, I might possibly allure some of my readers to familiarize themselves with these characters, by an application of them to the few words of those languages which are here introduced: and thus lead the way to their better acquaintance with the parent language, which ought long ago to have made a part of the education of our youth. And I flatter myself that one of the consequences of my present enquiry will be, to facilitate and abridge the tedious and mistaken method of instruction, which has too long continued in our seminaries: the time which is at present allotted to Latin and Greek. being amply sufficient for the acquirement also of French, Italian, Anglo-Saxon, Dutch, German, Danish and Swedish. Which will not seem at all extraordinary, when it is considered that the five last mentioned (together with the English) are little more than different dialects of one and the same language. *Ibid.* pp. 99–100.

THEORIES OF DERIVATION

[*If* derives from the Verb *Give*—i.e. grant—and all] conditional conjunctions are to be accounted for in ALL languages in the same manner. ... And the particular signification of each must be sought for amongst the other parts of Speech, by the help of the particular etymology of each respective language. By such means alone can we clear away the obscurity and errors in which Grammarians and Philosophers have been involved by the corruption of some common words, and the useful Abbreviations of Construction. And at the same time we shall get rid of that farrago of useless distinctions into Conjunctive, Adjunctive, Disjunctive [and some 3 dozen more] which explain nothing; and (as most other technical terms are abused) serve only to throw a veil over the ignorance of those who employ them.* *Ibid.* pp. 110–11.

* Technical terms are not invariably abused to cover the *ignorance* of those who employ them. In matters of law, politicks and Government, they are more frequently abused in attempting to impose upon the ignorance of *others*: and to cover the injustice and knavery of those who employ them.

Horne Tooke (1736–1812)

[Horne Tooke believes that *though* is from *þafian*, *algate* from *all-yet*, *without* from *weorðan*.]   *Ibid.* pp. 177, 173, 206.

S. Johnson calls "Thorough,—the word *Through* extended into two syllables". What could possibly be expected from such an Etymologist as this? He might, with as much verisimilitude, say that *saiwala*[1] was the word Soul extended into three syllables, or that Ελεημοσυνη[2] was the word Alms extended into six. [Johnson in fact was right. Horne Tooke thought *thorough* was the Teutonic substantive *Thuruh*, which means *door, gate, passage*.]   *Ibid.* p. 315, n.

NEATH, Neoðan, Neoðe (in the Dutch *Neden*, in the Danish *Ned*, in the German *Niedere*, and in the Swedish *Nedre* and *Neder*) is undoubtedly as much a substantive, and has the same meaning as the word NADIR: which Skinner (and after him S. Johnson) says, we have from the Arabians. This etymology (as the word is now applied only to astronomy) I do not dispute; but the word is much more ancient in the northern languages, than the introduction of that science among them. And therefore it was that the whole serpentine class was denominated Nadr[3] in the Gothic and Nedre[4] in the Anglo-Saxon.   *Ibid.* pp. 381–2.

NEEDS

*Need-is** used parenthetically. It was antiently written *Nedes* and *Nede is, Certain is* was used in the same manner, equivalently to *certes*.

Ibid. p. 449.

[Horne Tooke is good on words derived from Latin past participles: but he goes on to say that *odd* is the past participle of *owe*, *head* of *heave*, *wild* of *will* (=self-willed), *loud* of *low*, *thrift* of *thrive* and *gift* of *give*. *Field* land is opposed to woodland, and means land where the trees have been *felled*. *Bread* is derived from *Bray* (French *Broyer*, to pound): but

---

[1] [In Gothic characters.]   [2] [No accents.]   [3] [Gothic characters.]
[4] [Anglo-Saxon characters.]

* Mr Tooke does not seem to have been aware of the formation of adverbs from the genitive absolute, which prevails in the Teutonic languages: otherwise he would probably have given a different account of this word.
NEEDS, Genitive of Need, *of necessity*: as in German *Nachts*, by night, *Theils*, partly. [Footnote by Richard Taylor, editor of the 1829 edition.]

he knows that *Friend* and *Fiend* were originally present participles of verbs meaning to love and to hate. Aware that *it* was originally *hit*, he argues that *hit*=the past participle of *hatan*, to call.

He knows about the metathesis of R (giving many examples), which he uses to justify his derivation of *brawn* from *baren* (=*boaren*).

He sees that there is a connection between the noun and adjective *wrong* and the verb *wring*.

He thinks the participial endings -*en* and -*ed* were used indiscriminately.

Wench is the past participle of *Wink*—one may be had by a nod or a wink: he thinks it is a *k*/*ch* variant as in *speak, speech*; *Dike, Ditch*; *Drink, Drench*; *Stark, Starch*; *Kirk, Church*, in which pairs he does not see the real causes of variation.

Loaf is from *hlifian* to raise, so *Lord*=high born.

Day is the past participle of A.S. *dægian, lucescere*. By adding the participial termination -*en* to *dag*, we have *dagen* or DAWN.]

Ibid. vol. II, chs. 3, 4.

COMMON-SENSE DERIVATION

... I wish to know what you will do with Dryden's *Stitch-fall'n* cheek? [Trans. of the Tenth Satire of Juvenal].

Johnson says—"that perhaps it means *furrows* or *ridges*", and that "otherwise he does not understand it".

The woman who knitted his stockings could have told him, and explained the figure by her own mishap.   *Ibid.* p. 227.

BACK-TO-FRONT DERIVATION

[Horne Tooke assumes that *habere* derives from *haban* [*sic*], *sequi* from *secan, arare* from *erian, damnare* from *deman, petere* from *biddan*.]

Ibid. pp. 302–3.

[He gives examples of the pairing of English noun and foreign adjective—love, amorous; sleep, soporiferous; two, second:[1]]

The adoption of such words as these, was indeed a benefit and an improvement of our language; which however would have been much better and more properly obtained by *adjectiving* our own words. For, as the matter now stands, when a poor foreigner has learned all the names

[1] [His list includes some nouns not of native origin, and some words that are not nouns.]

of things in the English tongue, he must go to other languages for a multitude of the *adjectived names* of the *same things*. And even an unlearned native can never understand the meaning of one quarter of that which is called his native tongue.

Ibid. p. 448.

PRETERITE AND PAST PARTICIPLE

[Horne Tooke holds that] the Past Participle is merely the Past Tense Adjective: that it has merely the same meaning as the Past Tense, and no other; is most evident in English: because, in the same manner as we often *throw* one Noun substantive to another Noun substantive, without any change of termination to shew that it is so intended to be *thrown*; we are likewise accustomed to use the Past Tense itself without any change of termination, instead of this Past Participle; and the Past Tense so used, answers the purpose equally with the Participle, and conveys the same meaning. Dr. Lowth, who was much better acquainted with Greek and Latin than with English, . . . finds great fault with this our English custom; and complains that it . . . "is too much authorized by the example of some of our best writers." . . .

It is the idiom of the language.

Ibid. pp. 470–2 (quoted from the edition of 1829).

FRANCIS GROSE (1731?–1791)

PROVINCIAL WORDS

Provincial or local words are of three kinds, the first, either Saxon or Danish, in general grown obsolete from disuse, and the introduction of more fashionable terms, and consequently, only retained in countries remote from the capital, where modern refinements do not easily find their way, and are not readily adopted.

The second sort are words derived from some foreign language, as Latin, French, or German, but so corrupted by passing through the mouths of illiterate clowns as to render their origin scarcely discoverable; corruptions of this kind being obstinately maintained by country people, who, like the old Monks, will never exchange their old mumpsimus for the new sumpsimus.

The third are mere arbitrary words, not deducible from any primary

source of language, but ludicrous nominations, from some apparent qualities in the object or thing, at first scarcely current out of the parish, but by time and use extended over a whole county. Such are the Church-warden, Jack-sharp-nails, Crotch-tail, etc.[1]   *Provincial Glossary* (1787).
Preface, pp. iii–iv.

[Examples of the first sort are:]

AGATES,	On the way. N.[2]
AMELL,	Between, used in dividing time
ARVILL,	A funeral. N.
ATTERCOB,	A spider
BEER or BIRRE,	Force or Might. Chesh.
To BIG,	to build. Cumb.
To DIGHT,	to clean or dress
To DREE,	to hold out. N.
EAM,	Mine eam, my Uncle
FLYTE,	To scold or brawl. N.
RINE,	To touch or feel. N.
SACKLESS,	Innocent, faultless. N.
TOOM,	Empty
WANG-TOOTH,	The jaw-tooth
WARP,	To lay eggs. N.
WARY,	To curse. Lanc.
WARTH,	A water-ford
WRONG,	Crooked. Norf.

[Examples of the second sort are:]

ARK,	A large chest. Northumb.
AUMBRAY,	A pantry. N.
CORBY,	A crow. N.
FASH,	To trouble or teaze. N.
PLANCHING,	A wooden floor. Devonsh.
SEWENT or SUENT,	Even, regular, all alike. Exm[oor]
SLIM,	Wicked, malicious, perverse. N.
SPICE,	Raisins, plums, figs and such like fruit. Yks.

[1] [He defines these three words thus:]

CHURCHWARDEN	A shag, or cormarant. Suff.
JACK-SHARP-NAILS	A prickle-back, called also, in Middlesex, a strickleback. Derb.
CROTCH-TAIL	A kite.

[2] [N. means 'found in northern dialects'.]

Francis Grose (1731?–1791)

TEMSE,   A small sieve. N.

[Grose begins his Preface by stressing the 'utility of a Provincial Glossary to all persons desirous of understanding our ancient poets'; examples relevant to Shakespeare are:]

CREAM,   To mantle or froth. N.
EAGER, (Aigre) Sour, or tending to sourness, sometimes applied
       to the air. C.[1]
PADDOCK or PADDICK, A frog. N. & S.[2]
SNECK,   ... latch the door. N.
YARE,   nimble, ready, fit. Chaucer uses it for ready,
       quick, as does also Shakspear in the Tempest.

[Some of Grose's words are now listed in the Concise Oxford Dictionary with no suggestion that they are provincial:
dibble, bleb, canny, dingle, ajar, lad, lass, pet (a favourite), *to ted, tiny.*]

Ibid. passim.

NOAH WEBSTER (1758–1843)

ENGLISH IN AMERICA

Our modern grammars have done much more hurt than good. The authors have labored to prove, what is obviously absurd, viz. that our language is not made right; and in pursuance of this idea, have tried to make it over again, and persuade the English to speak by Latin rules, or by arbitrary rules of their own. Hence they have rejected many phrases of pure English, and substituted those which are neither English nor sense. Writers and Grammarians have attempted for centuries to introduce a subjunctive mode into English, yet without effect; the language requires none. . . . *Dissertations on the English Language with notes Historical and Critical to which is appended by way of Appendix an Essay on a Reformed Mode of Spelling* (Boston, 1789). Preface, p. vii.

[Webster approves of Horne Tooke's theories, and disapproves of such expressions as *a mean, averse from, if he have, he has gotten.*]
[It] is our business to find what the English language *is*, and not, how it *might have been made.* The most difficult task now to be performed by

---

[1] [C means 'common to several counties'.]
[2] [S means 'found in southern dialects'.]

135

the advocates of *pure English*, is to restrain the influence of men, learned in Greek and Latin, but ignorant of their own tongue. *Ibid.* p. ix.

[Johnson's] pedantry has corrupted the purity of our language, and [his] principles would in time destroy all agreement between the spelling and pronunciation of words. I once believed that a reformation of our o[r]thography would be unnecessary and impracticable. This opinion was hasty; being the result of a slight examination of the subject. I now believe with Dr. Franklin that such a reformation is practicable and highly *necessary*. *Ibid.* p. xi.

On examining the language, and comparing the practice of speaking among the yeomanry of this country, with the stile of Shakespear and Addison, I am constrained to declare that the people of America, in particular the English descendants, speak the most *pure English* now known in the world. There is hardly a foreign idiom in their language; by which I mean, a phrase that has not been used by the best English writers from the time of Chaucer. They retain a few obsolete *words*, which have been dropt by writers, probably from mere affectation, as those which are substituted are neither more melodious nor expressive. In many instances they retain correct phrases, instead of which the pretended refiners of the language have introduced those which are highly improper and absurd. . . .

The people of distant counties in England can hardly understand one another, so various are their dialects; but in the extent of twelve hundred miles in America, there are very few, I question whether a hundred words, except such as are used in employments wholly local, which are not universally intelligible. . . .

There is no Dictionary yet published in Great Britain, in which so many of the analogies of the language and the just rules of pronunciation are preserved, as in the common practice of the well informed Americans, who have never consulted any foreign standard. . . .

Ibid. Dissertation IV, pp. 288–90.

Our political harmony is concerned in a uniformity of language.

As an independent nation, our honor requires us to have a system of our own, in language as government. Great Britain, whose children we are, and whose language we speak, should no longer be *our* standard;

Noah Webster (1758–1843)

for the taste of her writers is already corrupted and her language on the decline. But if it were not so, she is at too great a distance to be our model, and to instruct us in the principles of our own tongue. . . . [For] within a century and a half, North America will be peopled with a hundred millions of men, *all speaking the same language.* [Isolation, new ideas, intercourse with native peoples] will produce, in a course of time, a language in North-America, as different from the future language of England, as the modern Dutch, Danish and Swedish are from the German, or from one another.

In many parts of America, people at present attempt to copy the English phrases and pronunciation. . . .

The Authors, who have attempted to give us a standard, make the practice of the court and stage in London the sole criterion of propriety in speaking. An attempt to establish a standard on this foundation is both *unjust* and *idle.*

The *general practice* of a nation is the rule of propriety. . . .

When a deviation from analogy has become the universal practice of a nation, it then takes place of all rules and becomes the standard of propriety.

It would have been fortunate for the language, had the stile of writing and the pronunciation of words been fixed, as they stood in the reign of Queen Ann [*sic*] and her successor.

[For Webster,] grammar is formed on language, not language on grammar.   *Ibid.* Dissertation I, pp. 20–37.

The primitive language of the English nation was the Saxon, and the words derived from that, now constitute the ground-work of modern English. Hence all the rules of inflection, and most of the rules of construction, are Saxon. . . . For this reason, the rules of grammatical construction and the propriety of particular phrases, can be ascertained only by the ancient Saxon, and the modern English writings. The Greek and Roman languages were constructed on different principles, which circumstance has not been sufficiently attended to, by those who have attempted to compile English Grammars.   *Ibid.* p. 61.

[Webster, in discussing pronunciation, says that some Americans give *angel* and *ancient* the *a* of angelic and antiquity.

Amongst errors, he mentions *marcy* for *mercy.*] The true sound of the short *e,* as in *let* is the correct and elegant pronunciation in all words of this class. [He thinks the name of the letter R has influenced the sound and so] to remedy the evil, this letter is named *er*, in the Institute. In a few instances this pronunciation is become general among polite speakers, as *clerks, sergeant.*

[*Skyi, gyide, kyind* represent] the elegant pronunciation of the fashionable people both in England and America. [Webster calls it barbarism.] Some of the southern people, particularly in Virginia, almost omit the sound of *r* as in *ware, there.* In the best English pronunciation, the sound of *r* is much softer than in some of the neighboring languages, particularly the Irish and Spanish. . . . But there seems to be no good reason for omitting the sound altogether. . . .

Chore, a corruption of *char,* is an English word, still used in many parts of England, as a *char-man,* a *char-woman,* but in America, it is perhaps confined to New England. It signifies small domestic jobs of work, and its place cannot be supplied by any other single word in the language.

The pronunciation of *w* for *v* is a prevailing practice in England and America. It is particularly prevalent in Boston and Philadelphia. Many people say *weal, wessel* for *veal, vessel* [This doesn't happen in Connecticut].

The words *shall, quality, quantity, qualify, quandary, quadrant,* are differently pronounced by good speakers.

Some give *a* a broad sound, as *shol, quolity*: and others, its second sound, as in *hat.*[1] With respect to the four first, almost all the standard writers agree to pronounce the *a* short as in *hat*: And this is the stage pronunciation. It is correct, for it is more agreeable to the analogy of the language. . . .

The words *either, neither, deceit, conceit, receipt,* are generally pronounced, by the eastern people, *ither, nither, desate, consate, resate.* These are errors; all the standard authors agree to give *ei,* in these words, the sound of *ee.* This is the practice in England, in the middle and southern states, and, what is higher authority, analogy warrants the practice.

[Webster disapproves of *Reesin* for *Raisin* and *Leesure* for *Lezhure.*] Our modern fashionable speakers accent *European* on the last syllable but one. This innovation has happened within a few years . . . it is a violation of an established principle . . . witness *Mediterránean, Pyrénean, Hercúlean, subterránean.*

Rome is very frequently pronounced *Room,* and that by people of

---

[1] [Webster provides a table of numbered vowels.]

every class. . . . It seems very absurd to give o its first[1] sound in *Romish*, *Romans*, and pronounce it *oo* in *Rome*, the radical word.

[The *h* in *wh-* words ought to be pronounced, Webster says, except in *who, whole, whoop, whore* and their derivatives. Presumably he means that these have *h* simply: it is not a question of a combination or particular sort of *w*.

Yuman is "a gross error".

H is silent in *herb* (and in English, in *hospital, hostler, humble*).

In *patriot, patriotism*, the English give *a* its long sound: but a great part of the Americans, its short sound.

Wrath is like *path* (in English like *wroth*).

Pierce rhymes with *rehearse*.

Deaf is generally pronounced *deef*.

Skeptic for *sceptic* is mere pedantry.

T ought not to become *tsh* in *Nature*, etc.]

Ibid. Dissertations II and III.

THE MOOD OF VERBS

It is astonishing to see how long and how stupidly English grammarians have followed the Latin grammars in their divisions of time and mode; but in particular the latter. By this means, we often find *may, can, should* and *must* in a conditional mode, when they are positive declarations and belong to the indicative. All unconditional declarations, whether of an action, or of a right, power or necessity of doing an action, belong to the indicative: and the distinction between the indicative and potential is totally useless.

Ibid. Dissertation IV, p. 231.

'YOU WAS'

In books, *you* is commonly used with the plural of the verb *be*, *you were*; in conversation, it is generally followed by the singular *you was*. Notwithstanding the criticisms of grammarians, the antiquity and universality of this practice must give it the sanction of propriety; for what but practice forms a language? This practice is not merely vulgar; it is general among men of erudition who do not affect to be fettered by the rules of grammarians, and some late writers have indulged it in their publications.

Ibid. pp. 233–4.

[1] [As in *note*.]

English Examined

NUMBER AND PERSON

Under this head, I shall remark on a single article only, the use of *you* in the singular number, with a plural verb. The use of the plural *nos* and *vos* for *ego* and *tu* in Latin; of *nous* and *vous* for *je* and *tu* in French; seems to have been very ancient, and to have been originally intended to soften the harshness of egotism, or to make a respectful distinction in favor of great personages. But the practice became general in the French nation, was introduced by them into England, and gradually imitated by the English in their own tongue. *You*, in familiar discourse, is applied to an individual, except by a single sect of christians; the practice is general and of long standing; it has become correct in English, and ought to be considered, in grammar, as a pronoun in the singular number.

Ibid. pp. 232–3.

CONFUSION OF 'SHALL' AND 'WILL'

I would just remark here, that the errors in the use of the auxiliary verbs [frequent in the Southern States] are not English; that they are little known among the inhabitants of South Britain, and still less among their descendants in New England. This is a new proof of the force of national customs. I do not remember to have heard once in the course of my life, an improper use of the verbs *will* and *shall*, among the unmixed English descendants in the eastern states.

Ibid. p. 240.

'WHO' AND 'WHOM'

"Who do you speak to?" "Who did he marry?" are challenged as bad English; but whom do you speak to? was never used in speaking, as I can find and if so, is hardly English at all. There is no doubt, in my mind, that the English *who* and the Latin *qui*, are the same word with mere variations of dialect. [As *cui* was sounded like *qui*, *who* is a good oblique case]. . . . Nay, it is more than probable that *who* was once wholly used in asking questions, even in the objective case; *who* did he marry? until some Latin student began to suspect it bad English, because not agreeable to the Latin rules. At any rate, *whom* do you speak to? is a corruption, and all the grammars that can be formed will not extend the use of the phrase beyond the walls of a college.

Ibid. pp. 286–7.

JOHN BRUCKNER (1726–1804)

CRITICISM OF HORNE TOOKE

[Horne Tooke asserts that the adj. *less* was the imperative of *lesan*, and the superlative *least* its past participle. John Bruckner comments as follows:]

You add in a note, It is the same imperative LES, placed at the end of nouns, and coalescing with them, which has given to our language such adjectives as HOPELESS, RESTLESS, DEATHLESS, MOTIONLESS. These words have been all along considered as compounds of *Hope, Rest,* &c. and the adjective *Less,* Anglo-Saxon *Leas,*[1] and Dutch *Loos*: and this explanation is so natural, so clear and satisfactory, that it is inconceivable how a man, who has any notion of neatness and consistency in etymological disquisitions, could ever think of their being compounds of a noun, and the imperative of the verb *Lesan.* LEAS and LOOS are still extant, this in the Dutch, and that in the Anglo-Saxon language; and both answer to the Latin *solutus* in this phrase *solutus cura.* So that *hopeless,* in the literal sense of the word, only means *void of hope; faithless, void of faith*; a sense so obvious, and so analogous to that which we mean to express when we use these words, that nothing but love of novelty in the extreme could induce you to reject it, in order to make room for the uncouth and awkward expressions *Hope-dismiss, Death-dismiss.* Where, in the name of wonder, have you ever found words tacked together in this manner?

Criticisms on 'The Diversions of Purley' (1790), p. 42.
By I. Cassander (John Bruckner's pseudonym).

METHODS OF FORMING COMPOUND WORDS

In all languages, as far as we know, which admit of composition in words, there is a certain manner which must be attended to, before we presume to make compounds; a manner in the arrangement; and a manner in the choice of those words which are to be joined together. Some are to be considered as prefixes, others as affixes; some will not coalesce; some, on the contrary, run into composition, as it were, of themselves. In this part of the structure, therefore, as well as in all the others, there is a kind of harmony, which must be attended to and serve as a rule. To take words at random and to jumble them together . . . is to

---

[1] [The Anglo-Saxon words are in Anglo-Saxon characters.]

violate that harmony: and this you do, when you tack an imperative to a noun for the purpose of making but one word of the two. . . . The French and the English have, indeed, their compounds of imperative and noun, but never of noun and imperative.* *Ibid.* p. 43.

But, supposing it was not, neither the French nor the modern English are, in that respect, a proper standard whereby we can determine the genius of the old language. *Ibid.*

IN DEFENCE OF DR JOHNSON

I cannot help taking notice here of the very extraordinary sentence you have been pleased to pass upon Johnson's Dictionary; a work which, now for many years, has been a kind of standard, by which even the most judicious, have ascertained the signification of words in the English language, and which therefore ought not to be depreciated, without giving weighty reasons for so doing. It has, no doubt, its blemishes: but they are not of the kind, *quas incuria fudit.* On the contrary, they may be called the result of the opposite cause, too much nicety and exactness. Had the author been less minute in distinguishing the various significations of words, he would have saved himself a great deal of trouble, and his work would not have been the worse for it. As it is, we have nothing better of the kind. The explanations are commonly just and clear; the quotations numerous, and from the best authorities: which inclines me to believe, that when you stigmatize it as a most contemptible performance, a reproach to the English nation, one third of it being as much the language of the Hottentots as of the English; you mean only to animadvert on such of the Doctor's definitions, divisions, and derivations, as do not perfectly coincide with your manner of dispatching that business.

[Bruckner takes Tooke to task for his "very curious" table of Anglo-Saxon verbs;] one third of which, if I may be allowed the expression, are of your own hatching, and some of them so cruelly mangled in the hatching, that they have not a limb left entire and in its place.

Beon-utan! *wyrðan-utan!* Mercy upon you for having found so much fault with others! *Ibid.* pp. 46–7.

---

* *Un coupe-jarret,* a banditto; *un boute-feu,* an incendiary; *un tire-bouchon,* a corkscrew. So in English, a cut-purse, a catch-penny &c. We say, indeed, a tooth-pick; but this is evidently corrupt from tooth-picker. [Actually, it is from the *noun* 'pick'.]

There is great reason to believe that Johnson and others have not mistaken the expression TO BOOT, when they called it a substantive; but that you were egregiously so, when you made an infinitive of it.[1]

Ibid. p. 60.

... there arises a strong presumption, that, if a few of your etymologies can bear examination, most of them cannot; being grounded on words, either not in the language, or not connected with those of which they are supposed to be the origin. *Ibid.* p. 73.

WILLIAM COBBETT (1763–1835)

THE USES OF GRAMMAR

Grammar, perfectly understood, enables us, not only to express our meaning fully and clearly, but so to express it as to enable us to defy the ingenuity of man to give to our words any other meaning than that which we ourselves intend them to express. This, therefore, is a science of substantial utility.

A Grammar of the English Language in a Series of Letters
(New York, 1818), Letter II, 3 (quoted from
the edition published in London, 1819).

SUNDRY COMMENTS

[He thinks men, women, to be plurals in -en.] *Ibid.* Letter V, 41.

Thou is here given as the *second person singular*; but, common custom has set aside the rules of Grammar in this case; and, though we, in particular cases, still make use of *Thou* and *Thee*, we generally make use of *You* instead of either of them. According to ancient rule and custom this is not correct; but, what a whole people adopts and universally practises, must, in such cases, be deemed correct, and to be a superseding of ancient rule and custom. *Ibid.* Letter VI, 57.

---

[1] [Tooke thinks there is a verb *bote* (to superadd) and that *boot* is its imperative. Bruckner shows that *bot* is a noun meaning recompense or fine, and *to bote* means *into the bargain*. *To bote* in Anglo-Saxon could not be an infinitive, but has the characteristic dative sign.]

Perhaps a profound examination of the matter would lead to a proof of *That* being always a pronoun; but, as such examination would be more curious than useful, I shall content myself with having clearly shown you the difference in its offices as a *relative*, as a *demonstrative*, and as a *conjunction*.[1]

Ibid. 68.

[Cobbett objects to the historical shortened vowel in such preterites and past participles as *meant*, and to the strong forms of e.g.—*blow, freeze, swim*, and uses the weak forms in the *Grammar*.]

Ibid. Letter VIII, 108.

The frequent use of abbreviation is always a mark of slovenliness and of vulgarity. I have known Lords abbreviate almost the half of their words: it was, very likely, because they did not know how to spell them to the end.

Ibid. Letter XIV, 153.

NOUNS OF MULTITUDE

Nouns of number, or multitude, such as *Mob, Parliament, Rabble, House of Commons, Regiment, Court of King's Bench, Den of Thieves*, and the like, may have pronouns agreeing with them either in the singular or in the plural number: . . . The rule is this: that nouns of multitude *may* take *either* the singular, or the plural, pronoun; but not *both* in the same sentence.

Ibid. Letter XVII, 181.

EXAGGERATION

"*Very* right" and "*very* wrong", are very common expressions, but they are both incorrect. Some expressions may be *more common* than others; but that which is *not right* is *wrong*; and that which is *not wrong* is *right*. There are here no intermediate degrees. We should laugh to hear a man say, "you are a *little* right, I am a *good deal wrong*; that person is honest in *a trifling degree*; that act was *too* just." But, our ears are accustomed to the adverbs of exaggeration. Some writers deal in these to a degree that tries the ear and offends the understanding. With them, everything

[1] [This seems the appropriate comment on Horne Tooke's 'demonstration' in *The Diversions of Purley* that *that* is always a Pronoun.]

William Cobbett (1763–1835)

is *excessively* or *immensely* or *vastly* or *surprisingly* or *wonderfully* or *abundantly*, or the like. The notion of such writers is, that these words give *strength* to what they are saying. This is a great error. Strength must be found in the *thought*, or it will never be found in the *words.* Big-sounding words, without thoughts corresponding, are effort without effect.

Ibid. Letter XVIII, 220.

ENGLISH AND LATIN

In the Latin language, the Verbs change their endings so as *to include in the Verbs themselves* what we express by our auxiliary verb *to have*. And they have as many changes, or different endings, as are required to express all those various circumstances of time that we express by, *work, worked, shall work, may work, might work, have worked, had worked, shall have worked, may have worked, might have worked*; and so on. It is, therefore, necessary for the Latins to have distinct appellations to suit these various circumstances of time, or states of an action; but, such distinction of appellations can be of no use to *us*. . . .

Why, then, should we perplex ourselves with a multitude of artificial distinctions, which cannot, by any possibility, be of any use in practice? These distinctions have been introduced from this cause: those who have written English Grammars, have been taught Latin; and, either unable to divest themselves of their Latin rules, or unwilling to treat with simplicity that, which, if made somewhat of a mystery, would make them appear more *learned* than the mass of the people, they have endeavoured to make our simple language turn and twist itself so as to become as complex in its principles as the Latin language is.

Ibid. Letter XIX, 256–7.

PRETERITE AND PARTICIPLE

You often hear people say, and see them write, "We *have spoke*; it *was spoke* in my hearing;" But, "we *have came*; it *was did*," are just as correct.

Ibid. 263.

[Cobbett thinks that 'If he *work*' is short for 'If he *should work*', and that 'work' is therefore an infinitive.]   *Ibid.* 274.

145

ANONYMOUS (early nineteenth century)

CORRECT LETTER-WRITING

1. ORTHOGRAPHY . . . is of the highest importance; ignorance in this particular is always considered a mark of ill-breeding, defective education, or natural stupidity. To attain this it is necessary to observe the method followed by the best writers of the present day, and to consult some good modern Dictionary, such as those of Johnson and Walker, Brown's Union Dictionary, Jones's Sheridan, etc. . . .

2. GRAMMAR is deduced from certain rules, the observation of which is essential to perspicuity, as well as to correctness. Murray's Grammar (or his Abridgement) is now most generally used; but all agree in the most essential points. The rules cannot be here introduced, but the following are some of the most glaring faults committed by uneducated persons; *I comes, I goes,* for *I come* or *go*; *you loves, you hates,* instead of *you love* or *hate. Learn* is frequently used for *teach, set* for *sit, lay* for *laid, mistaken* for *mistaking,* and persons from the north frequently confound *shall* and *will, would* and *should.* Adjectives are often used for adverbs, as he "wrote *agreeable,*" instead of "he wrote agreeably"; it is *remarkable* ugly, instead of "remarkably ugly". The subjunctive mood is little attended to even by some persons who have learned Grammar; hence they say, "If he *was*", instead of "If he *were*," etc. . . .

4. PUNCTUATION, in as much as it is necessary to the proper division of sentences, is of great importance to perspicuity. . . . In general, points are the pauses which a correct orator would use in speaking; and as a knowledge of their power is to be acquired with a little care, the neglect of them is unpardonable. *The London Universal Letter-Writer* (n.d.). Introduction, pp. 1–3.

[From the model letter of a Preceptor to his Scholar.]

Never let me see you write *you was,* or I shall deny *you were* ever a pupil of mine. Be attentive to the time, and do not jumble the present, past and future, as many writers do. Use the conditional mode, provided the sentence *be* conditional: this, I confess, is not a general observation; but if a man *pretend* to write, he ought to be correct. Do not crowd us with monosyllables, for they are very insignificant creatures; nor use many long words, for fear you may exceed comprehension. I hate

Anonymous (early nineteenth century)

particles where they are avoidable; be therefore sparing in your *fors*, your *buts*, and your *ands*. . . . Do not arrogate the power of making words, for we have sufficient in our language to express our meaning, and there are few who possess competent abilities for the task. Avoid cant and obsolete phrases. . . .

Ibid. p. 19.

APPENDIX I

A reference list of important comment in the major authors
whose works are easily accessible

1. BEN JONSON (1572–1637).
Edition by C. H. Herford, Percy and Evelyn Simpson (Oxford, at the
Clarendon Press, 1947).
Vol. IV: *The Poetaster*, Act V, Sc. iii: on hard and unpoetical words.
Vol. VIII: *The English Grammar*: on style, pp. 615–18; on appropriate
words, pp. 261, 625–8; on custom, p. 622; on letter-writing, pp. 629–
33.

2. THOMAS HOBBES (1588–1679).
Leviathan (1651) (conveniently in the Everyman edition). Part I,
Chapter 4, 'Of Speech', includes comment on word definition, and
on the dangers of misleading Greek and Latin terms. Chapter 5: on
inconsistent ideas veiled in words, and on dangerous metaphor. Chapter 6: "The formes of Speech by which the Passions are expressed".
The Virtues of an Heroic Poem: in Spingarn: on diction, vol. II, p. 68.

3. JOHN DRYDEN (1631–1700).
Essays of John Dryden, selected and edited by W. P. Ker (Oxford,
Clarendon Press, 1926).
Preface to *Annus Mirabilis* (1666). On new words, vol. I, pp. 17–18.
The Rival Ladies (1664): the need for an Academy, vol. I, p. 5. *An
Essay of Dramatic Poesy* (1668): on the nobility of English, vol. I, p. 104.
An Essay of the Dramatic Poetry of the Last Age (1672): linguistic faults,
vol. I, pp. 164–9; French affectations, vol. I, p. 170; changes of mean-
ing, vol. I, p. 171. Preface to the Translation from Ovid's *Epistles*
(1680): difficulties of translating and borrowing from Latin, vol. I,
pp. 237 ff. Preface to *Sylvæ* (1685): current ignorance of the niceties
of English, p. 253; dialect in poetry, vol. I, pp. 265–6. Preface to
Albion and Albanius (1685): the qualities of English, French, and Italian,
vol. I, p. 274. *Examen Poeticum* (1693): faults of English, vol. II, p. 12.
Preface to *The Fables* (1700): on Chaucer, vol. II, pp. 248–9.
For satire on affected French loans, see also *Marriage à la Mode*, Act II,
i and III, i and *Sir Martin Mar-all*, Act III, i.

4. JOHN LOCKE (1632–1704).
Conveniently in the Everyman edition (last reprint 1959): edited A. C. Fraser (2 vols. Oxford, 1894).
An Essay concerning Human Understanding. Book III: 'Of Words'. Especially ch. II, 2, on the relation between words and ideas; ch. II, 8, on the arbitrariness of language; ch. v, 7, on words for complex ideas; 8, on 'intranslatable words'; ch. VII, 'Of Particles'[1]; ch. VIII, 'Of abstract and Concrete Terms'; ch. IX, 'Of the Imperfections of Words', and ch. x, 'Of the Abuse of Words'.

5. JONATHAN SWIFT (1667–1745).
Hints towards an Essay on Conversation and *Polite Conversations* are in the Everyman volume entitled *The Tale of a Tub.*
The *Conversations* (*Tatler*, no. 230) and the *Letter to a young Clergyman* are in the Oxford Standard Authors volume of Satires and Personal Writings. These, and the Letter to the Lord High Treasurer proposing the establishment of an Academy, are in vol. XI of the Temple-Scott edition of Swift (Bell and Sons, 1907).

6. PHILIP DORMER STANHOPE, LORD CHESTERFIELD (1694–1773).
The Letters to his Son are most easily accessible in the Everyman Library. References by page to the first (1929) edition, which was last reprinted in 1957. On oratory, p. 3: 1 November 1739; vulgarism, p. 10, pp. 122–3: 25 July, N.S. 1741, 27 September, O.S. 1749; awkwardness in speech, p. 11: 6 August 1741; good conversation, p. 34: 16 October, O.S. 1747; inelegant writing and diction, pp. 133–4, 137: 24 November, O.S. 1749 and 5 December, O.S. 1749; spelling, pp. 203–4: 19 November, O.S. 1750.

7. DR SAMUEL JOHNSON (1709–84).
The *Plan* and *Preface* of the Dictionary are in the Reynard Library Johnson, published by Hart-Davis, and in the volume of Philological Tracts in Murphy's collected edition.
The *Idler* (1761): no. 36, The Terrifick Diction; no. 63, Progress of Arts and Language; no. 68 and no. 69, History of Translations; no. 70, Hard Words Defended; no. 77, Easy Writing; no. 91, Sufficiency of the English Language.
The *Rambler* (1750–2): no. 94, relation of sense and sound; no. 121, on Spenser's diction; no. 140, on Milton's diction; no. 168, on low words.

[1] [Not in *Everyman* Edition.]

APPENDIX II

Passages of special importance in (a) J. E. Spingarn, *Critical Essays of the 17th Century* (Oxford, Clarendon Press, 1908); (b) W. H. Durham, *Critical Essays of the 18th Century* (Yale U.P., 1915)

(*a*)

John Evelyn to Sir Peter Wyche (1665), vol. II, pp. 310–13: proposals for reforming and codifying English.

Thomas Sprat, *History of the Royal Society* (1667): proposal for erecting an English Academy, vol. II, pp. 112–15; plain English, the Society's ideal, vol. II, pp. 116–19.

Joseph Glanvill, *An Essay concerning Preaching* (1678): plain English and pure English, vol. II, pp. 273–5.

Robert Wolseley, Preface to Rochester's *Valentinian*: on loss of syllables, vol. III, pp. 26–7.

William Wotton, *Of Ancient and Modern Grammar*: vol. III, pp. 223–6.

(*b*)

John Hughes, *Of Style* (1698): p. 79.

John Dennis, *Reflections upon a Late Rhapsody*: p. 233.

Pope, Preface to *The Iliad* (1715): on translation and the choice of poetic diction, pp. 342–6.

Leonard Welsted, *The State of Poetry* (1724): perfection in language, pp. 358 ff.

APPENDIX III

Brief details of the authorities quoted

JOSEPH ADDISON, essayist and politician, 1672–1719.

EDWARD BREREWOOD, theologian and historian, 1565?–1613.

SIR THOMAS BROWNE, physician and philosopher, 1605–82.

JOHN BRUCKNER, Lutheran divine settled at Norwich, 1726–1804.

JAMES BURNETT, LORD MONBODDO, Scottish judge, anthropologist, 1714–99.

RICHARD OWEN CAMBRIDGE, poet and essayist, 1717–1802.

WILLIAM CAMDEN, herald and antiquary, 1551–1623.

ARCHIBALD CAMPBELL, naval purser, 1726?–80.

LORD CHESTERFIELD, statesman and aristocrat, 1694–1773.

WILLIAM COBBETT, soldier, farmer, member of Parliament, reformer, 1763–1835.

CHRISTOPHER COOPER, grammarian and phonetician, *fl.* 1685.

DANIEL DEFOE, business man, secret agent, journalist, novelist, 1660?–1731.

WILLIAM DRAKE, antiquary and schoolmaster, 1723–1801.

JOHN DRYDEN, poet and critic, 1631–1700.

THOMAS DYCHE, schoolmaster and lexicographer, *fl.* first quarter of the eighteenth century.

ELIZABETH ELSTOB, Anglo-Saxonist, 1683–1756.

LAURENCE EUSDEN, poet-laureate, 1688–1730.

GEORGE FOX, founder of the Society of Friends, 1624–91.

BENJAMIN FRANKLIN, statesman and scientist, 1706–90.

JOSEPH GLANVILL, philosopher, 1636–80.

JAMES GREENWOOD, schoolmaster and grammarian, *ob.* 1737.

FRANCIS GROSE, antiquary and draughtsman, 1731?–91.

JAMES HARRIS, country gentleman and politician, 1709–80.

PETER HEYLIN, religious controversialist, 1600–62.

GEORGE HICKES, linguist, non-juror, 1642–1715.

THOMAS HOBBES, philosopher, 1588–1679.

WILLIAM HOLDER, divine, musician, teacher of deaf-mutes, 1616–98.

JAMES HOWELL, letter writer and traveller, 1594?–1666.

GEORGE JEFFREYS, poet and critic, 1678–1755.

SAMUEL JOHNSON, critic and lexicographer, 1709–84.

BEN JONSON, poet and dramatist, 1572–1637.

HAMON L'ESTRANGE, historian and theologian, 1605–60.

WILLIAM L'ISLE, Esquire of the King's Body, Saxonist, 1569?–1637.

JOHN LOCKE, philosopher, 1632–1704.

ROBERT LOWTH, bishop and grammarian, 1710–87.

JAMES MARRIOTT, lawyer, politician and writer, 1730?–1803.

JEREMIAH MILLES, Dean of Exeter, 1714–84.

EDWARD MOORE, editor and essayist, 1712–57.

ARTHUR MURPHY, dramatist and journalist, 1727–1805.

THOMAS PERCY, bishop and antiquarian, 1729–1811.

ALEXANDER POPE, poet and critic, 1688–1744.

LORD SHAFTESBURY, statesman and philosopher, 1671–1713.

THOMAS SHERIDAN, elocutionist, 1719–88.

RICHARD STEELE, dramatist, essayist, and Member of Parliament, 1672–1729.

JONATHAN SWIFT, critic, satirist, politician and churchman, 1667–1745.

HORNE TOOKE, philologist and political agitator, 1736–1812.

THOMAS TYRWHITT, classical and Chaucerian scholar, Clerk to the House of Commons, 1730–86.

RICHARD VERSTEGAN, alias ROWLANDS, antiquary, *fl.* 1565–1620.

WILLIAM WALKER, schoolmaster, 1623–84.

JOHN WALLIS, grammarian and mathematician, 1616–1703.

THOMAS WARTON, literary historian and poet, 1728–90.

ISAAC WATTS, divine and educationist, 1674–1748.

NOAH WEBSTER, American lexicographer, 1758–1843.

JOHN WESLEY, religious reformer, 1703–91.

JOHN WILKINS, bishop, linguistic philosopher, mathematician, 1614–72.

Ephraim Chambers's *Cyclopaedia of Arts and Sciences*
The World
The Universal London Letter-writer

Except for Defoe, for whom recent criticism favours 1660, and for Bruckner and Holder, for whom I have consulted the *Dictionary of National Biography*, the dates and spellings follow the authority of *The Cambridge Bibliography of English Literature* and *The Oxford Companion to English Literature*.

SELECT INDEX

Index

154